'Brilliant! Jam-packed  every page. Encouragement ev... for happiness and start following your joy!'

Robert Holden Ph.D., Author of *Happiness NOW* and *Shift Happens!*

'The world's greats, those who are truly brilliant, make the impossible a ...ossible and the complex, simple; Messi can dribble, Branson c... ...e and Picasso could doodle. Cope and Whittaker distil the complexity of life like no other authors today; their charm, insight, wit and wisdom is touching, provoking and achingly funny. Read this and being brilliant every day will be . . . a doddle!'

Richard Gerver, Speaker, Author and Broadcaster

'[NOT read this book – it's far too good and it's making me insanely jealous'

David Taylor, Author of *The Naked Leader*

'HAPPY'

(By 9-year-old Aaron, who attended 'The Art of Being Brilliant' at his school. He just happens to be dyslexic.)

Choose to be happy
Sadness never got you anything
When you start to feel sad
Just remember friends and family
And kind strangers too
All support you.
Look on the bright side
At least you have a family.

When I am sad
And need cheering up
I run around with my dog
And eat lovely food.
Back flips, front flips
Trampoline bouncing
These make me happy and glad
To always be me.

BE BRILLIANT EVERY DAY

Use the power of positive psychology to make an impact on life

Andy Cope and Andy Whittaker
Illustrations by Laura E. Martin

CAPSTONE
A Wiley Brand

Registered office
John Wiley and Sons Ltd, The Atrium, Southern Gate, Chichester, West Sussex, PO19 8SQ, United Kingdom

For details of our global editorial offices, for customer services and for information about how to apply for permission to reuse the copyright material in this book please see our website at www.wiley.com.

Library of Congress Cataloging-in-Publication Data is available

A catalogue record for this book is available from the British Library.

ISBN 978-0-857-08500-9 (pbk) ISBN 978-0-857-08498-9 (ebk)
ISBN 978-0-857-08499-6 (ebk)

Cover design by Mackerel Ltd

Set in 10/14 pt FrutigerLTStd-Light by Toppan Best-set Premedia Limited
Printed in Great Britain by Bell and Bain, Thornliebank, Glasgow

MIX
Paper from
responsible sources
FSC www.fsc.org **FSC® C015829**

For Lightning-Legs Whittaker, Scrump and Bwana

CONTENTS

Sandy had made a decision to do
something with her life. She was going
to bloody well ENJOY IT!

ANDY AND ANDY'S BIG DAY OUT

Andy W's from Mansfield and I'm from Derby. So we're always excited to get an invite to London. And it's doubly exciting to be going to a meeting with our publishers.

Andy's not allowed on the underground on his own, not after the last time, so I held his hand on the Tube. We ascended the escalator, Andy standing in the middle, innocently blocking the rushy people. I got to the barrier, inserted my ticket and the gate opened. I was through. But Andy wasn't. And he was looking nervous. Sure, they have recently started having trains in Mansfield but not ones that live underground. And there aren't any moving staircases. And they certainly don't have electronic swishy gates.

He inserted his ticket. *Nothing*. I could see the panic in his eyes. A queue started building up so I summoned a guy in a London Underground hat. He opened the gate with his cool key fob and Andy fell through. The man in the hat examined Andy's ticket and looked my co-author in the eye. 'Thick cut,' I think he said.

We emerged, mole-like, blinking in the brightness of the overground. The city was a blur.

We had an hour to kill so we made our way to Starbucks. Double espresso for me and a sparkling water for Andy. He's not allowed coffee. Not after last time. 'In fact, make it a still water.'

And we made our way to the meeting. We'd rehearsed. I was going to do all the talking. (Andy W wasn't allowed, *not after last time* . . .)

Our instructions were clear. Yes, Capstone wanted another book. *Yippee!* 'But do NOT write a book about happiness,' said our publisher. 'Or, at least, if you do, don't *say* that it's a book about happiness. Hide it.'

Our publisher explained that 'happiness' has gone and got itself a bad name. Its wishy-washy pink fluffiness turns people off apparently. The 'happiness' brand is tarnished. He reeled off some stats. People are more likely to buy books about how to be 'confident' or 'optimistic' or 'lucky' and especially 'stinking rich'. 'In fact, what a great idea. Why don't you and Andy write a book called *The Art of Becoming Stinking Rich*? Even if it's rubbish, you'll shift a million copies!' He grinned at us as the irony sank in. '*Thereby becoming stinking rich!*'

Andy W gave me one of his looks. He started fidgeting and his eyes were gleaming. He's not very good at bottling things up and I thought it best to give him the nod, before he exploded with enthusiasm. 'It'll be a book about "wealth",' he blurted, a broad smile spreading across his chops. 'In its *widest* sense.'

Because Andy knows, like you and I know, that money is nice. And it's useful in smoothing the path to having a superb life. But 'wealth' is what you have left over after all your money's run out. Wealth is a measure of life that involves more than your bank account. Because 'wealth' is about true riches. It encompasses relationships, emotions, habits, health, happiness and all the lovely trappings that philosophers say 'money can't buy'.

So, this book does contain some stuff about happiness . . . and so much more. Read it. Apply the principles. Our aim is not to make you rich. It's much bolder than that.

Nine-year-old Aaron's poem nailed it. We want to make you wealthy beyond your wildest dreams.

Reg wondered if anyone would ever claim what was rightfully theirs

THE TINKER MAN

'If you think education is expensive, try ignorance.'
Vidal Sassoon

C helsea Football Club used to have a manager called Claudio Ranieri, affectionately known as 'The Tinker Man'. He kept tweaking the team, looking for small improvements.

And I guess this book is similar. It's for the tinkerers – the ones who dare to tweak and change things about themselves in the quest to be better. It's also for those who've read other personal development books and found them too earnest, difficult, pious or simple. It's for those who want to seize the moment, who are not afraid of hard work and who refuse to snuggle down on the wonderfully inviting bed of excuses.

Although this book falls into the 'personal development' genre, my sneaky suspicion is that you probably haven't got massive 'problems'. At least, no more 'problems' than Andy and I have. You'll have issues with feeling knackered a lot. You'll have more pressure at work than ever before. Your weeks will be flashing by far too rapidly. You'll be frustrated that your kids sometimes irk you. You'll be dragged down when you're surrounded by negative people. When you catch your naked reflection in the mirror you'll be noticing some imperfections. But they're not really 'problems'. They're just 'life'.

On the other hand, you might be drawn to this book because you're *not* feeling very brilliant. There will be times in everyone's life when things get on top of them. In which case, I'm confident you'll find this book helpful. It's a reminder that we all have brilliance within us. It's just that sometimes it's hidden behind a big bag of bad habits. Or sometimes life just throws so much shit at you that some of it sticks. In which case, think of this book as your very own personal face cloth.

I recently went to a university reunion and met up with Clive. He'd ballooned in weight, from a lithe, sporty, football-mad student to a bloated, 23-stone, middle-aged manager. I was rather taken aback and, after having my confidence stiffened and my tact loosened by a couple of beers, I asked him what had happened to 'Slim Clive'. He looked at me with a big, wobbly face and said, almost greedily, 'I've eaten him'.

So there's a lovely slim Clive fighting to get out! Now, I'm not going to get into the debate about who or what made Clive fat. Clive happens to think it's his job. He travels a lot with work and is always staying in hotels where the sausage and bacon are calling him. '*Come here Clivey. You've a big day ahead and you never know where your next meal's coming from, so fill up baby. Come to daddy.*'

So Clive was pretty much like I used to be. For 35 years, there was a brilliant Andy – *inside*. I kept him hidden. I'd shine sporadically. So I guess this book is for the old me. The muddling through, self-doubting, quietly unconfident me.

At its heart, this book isn't really about changing who you are. It's about being more and more of who you already are when you're at your brilliant best. It's about coming alive. Because that's what the world needs. Too many people are conforming to what they *think* the world needs whereas the reality is that what the world needs is simply the awesome version of you.

Before we crack on, just a couple of sentences about our content and style.

First of all, is the work in this book original? In places, yes. A lot of the themes are based on my thesis, parts of which are appearing in print for the first time. You can't get 'newer' or more 'original' than that. But, fair's fair, I agree that significant chunks of it aren't original. I guess what we're attempting to do is dig out interesting material and present it in a way that it's never been presented before.

This book isn't a step-by-step guide to inner happiness or millionaire status. Nor will it provide a concrete list of things you have to go away and practise. It's a little more ethereal in the sense that we will present 'This is what the science says' . . . and it's for you to . . . *now go away and make of it what you will.* The aim is to make you think about *how* you think.

We've all seen bags of peanuts that contain a warning, 'might contain nuts'. And in Toys-R-Us I saw a child's Superman cape that came with a warning; 'Wearing of this garment doesn't allow you to fly'.

In a similar vein, we reckon it's OK to have a positive mind-set, but let's not go too far. Let's not be ridiculous about positivity.

There are many instances where it's appropriate to be downbeat, cautious and pessimistic. There are some jobs where negative thinking is actually a requirement. If I was recruiting pilots for British Airways I would go out of my way to select cautious, risk-averse, negative people. As a passenger, the last thing I want is to be taxiing on the runway when there's a bing bong, *'This is your captain speaking. Air traffic control have said it's too icy to take off but, do you know what, I thought I'd give it a go.'*

No thanks. That's the dangerous cloud-cuckoo end of the positivity spectrum. We're positioned a notch or two down from there at the 'optimistic but realistic' end. The part of the spectrum that allows you to stand out a mile for the right reasons. The exact point on the 'brill-ometer' of being your best self, *consistently* and *appropriately*.

It's also worth noting that we have a rather self-deprecating style. (I've warned Andy W not to confuse that with 'self-defecating'. That'd just be awkward.) Ultimately, we thought, let's just write something that *we* enjoy. Something that's fun and makes us giggle like a pair of schoolboys.

While on the topic of humour, it also begs the question, is 'self-help' a laughing matter? A lot of personal development can be rather earnest because, I guess, ultimately, life is a serious business. A fellow trainer warned us against being too light and frivolous. People reading this might be depressed or suicidal or in the depths of despair. If you are, quite frankly, the last thing you need is a heavy tome. You're much better off having a chuckle.

But be careful folks, even humour can be a form of self-harming. Someone once died laughing at *The Goodies* (for the younger generation, *The Goodies* was a madcap 1970s TV show. Google it.) We know the following is true because it's on Wikipedia.

On 24 March, 1975, Alex Mitchell, from King's Lynn, England, died laughing while watching the 'Kung Fu Kapers' episode. It featured a kilt-clad Scotsman with his bagpipes battling against a master of the Lancastrian martial art 'Eckythump', who was armed with a black pudding.

After 25 minutes of continuous laughter, Mitchell finally slumped on the sofa and died from heart failure.

Obviously, someone dying isn't funny, per se. But someone dying laughing? We've all got to pop off at some point and in the grand scheme of ways to pop off, it's got to be up there.

In the modern world *The Goodies* would have been banned and Tim Brooke-Taylor, Graeme Garden and Bill Oddie hauled up in court to be sued by the family for 'damages'.

So it warmed my cockles to find out (again, from Wikipedia) 'His widow later sent *The Goodies* a letter thanking them for making Mitchell's final moments of life so pleasant.'

Now, we're not intending that you'll laugh so much that you die (although if you do, please send us a nice letter not a court summons), but we do want to make you grin.

And, to paraphrase Stan from *South Park* . . . just because we laugh doesn't mean we don't care.

I think personal development boils down to various flavours. There's 'cheesy cliché' flavour. You know the sort. 'Winners never give up'. *What, never ever?*

Then there's the 'heavyweight medicinal' books that you struggle through as if they've got some magic healing powers. Andy and I call these books 'academic porn'. *'Whisper me those big words, baby. You know, the ones I don't understand.'*

Or 'sugary advice' flavour. 'Live every day like it was your last'. *What, in a hospital bed, being leered at by 14 close family members?*

And there's good old 'All-American Apple Pie' flavour, which involves a lot of punching the air and asking gung-ho questions like, 'What would you do if you knew you couldn't fail?' But the voice inside you says, *'But I can fail. And I do. Often!'*

Or classic, best-selling 'soulful chicken soup' flavour – hearty and warming, if, dare I say, a bit rich?

So what flavour are we? I'd love to be able to say this book is tangy, zesty and full of fizz. But I'd be fibbing. This book is good, old-fashioned 'common sense' flavour. It's got quite an earthy, realistic taste to it. It acknowledges that most people are simply exhausted by modern life. You may well be stuck in a job you don't particularly like, or have an irksome manager, and you'd like to jack it all in but you can't. Most people have responsibilities, mortgages, mouths to feed and satellite TV to subscribe to. The weather can be a bit grim and the cost of living is out-stripping the cost of surviving.

> 'Some mornings, it's just not worth chewing through the leather straps.'
>
> *Emo Philips*

So our book may be 'earthy', but it's by no means bland, because there's another strand of personal development that is currently undergoing something of a renaissance – the broadly Eastern philosophy that encompasses the meditative 'living in the now' school of thought. So we've added a liberal sprinkling of 'Eastern Promise' to our earthy, common-sense approach. And you'll notice just a dash of something else, a certain *je ne sais quoi* that you can't quite place.

In short, we've devoured every personal development book on the planet, so you don't have to! We've garnered the very best of what we know and attempted to present it in the most palatable way we can.

Bon appetit!

FORGET 'SELF-IMPROVEMENT', TRY 'SELF-REMEMBERING'

'There is nothing better for self-growth than someone challenging your own viewpoint.'

Richard Gerver

If you're of a certain age, you'll remember Victor Kiam's Remington advert. For those too young to remember, Victor loved his razor so much that he bought the company, which, I have to admit, is kind of cool.

Victor Kiam is to Remington what I am to positive psychology. I love the subject so much I bought into it and have, so far, invested 10 years of my life in study, culminating in a PhD.

I appreciate that you can know *too* much. People can become nerdy in their subject knowledge. You can, for instance, develop an unhealthy interest in trains. Or moths. And it can also happen with personal development. I acknowledge that I'm at the nerdy end of the spectrum. Thankfully, Andy W isn't clever enough to be a geek, so he keeps me grounded with comments like *'Be careful boss, you're disappearing up your own backside again.'* Thanks Andy.

Studying, for me, is a strange combination of joy and struggle. For the first four years of study I simplified things and presented my PhD findings in flowing language that your average human being would want to read. I presented pages and pages of lucid and entertaining material. And I was perplexed because my academic supervisor would tut. '*Not academic enough.*' So I'd go away and make it more complex. And I'd come back and she'd tut again.

It wasn't until fairly recently that my PhD tutor confided that my aim should be to write in such a complicated way that she has to read everything three times to fathom it. Four or five times would be even better. If she couldn't understand it at all, that'd be perfect. And the penny dropped. I have to go beyond nerdy. It's a game. I have to torpedo the science of happiness and sink it to 100 fathoms.

And, speaking of fathoms, I liken it to pearl diving. First of all, oysters reside on the sea bed and are very well sealed, which makes them hard to access. Plus, only one oyster per hundred has a pearl. So that's a lot of effort to find something worthwhile. For me, studying at this level is taking a lot of effort and I have spent a great deal of time opening up worthless lines of inquiry. But, just occasionally, I come across a pearl. And that's what this book is about – sharing the pearls of wisdom.

You're probably familiar with the principle of parsimony.

No, me neither. At least not until recently. Sometimes called 'Occam's Razor', it states that among competing hypotheses, the hypothesis with the fewest assumptions should be selected. In plain, simple English, the simplest theory is usually the better one.

Oh boy, do I love Occam's Razor!

Let me give you an example of when I went too nerdy and Andy W nailed it. A couple of years back, we were guest speakers at an audiologists' conference. Lovely people. They fit hearing aids and do some marvellous life-changing stuff. But if you boil their job down to the basics, they spend a lot of time shining lights into people's ears. And they've all got Masters degrees and doctorates in this, that and the other. So I prepared a talk that I thought would engage them. I made sure it was pitched at the clever end of the spectrum with lots of detail and some stats. And I bored the pants off them.

Next up was Andy '*Occam's Razor*' Whittaker, distilling everything down to its very simplest form. In his own seemingly effortless way, he sold the science of happiness to them with an opening line something akin to, '*Look here you lot, if you're looking into my lug holes, I want you to be doing it with a smile on your face.*'

And, I have to say, that made a lot more sense.

A paradigm shift is when you suddenly see things in a different way. Most other books use flat-Earth thinking or Roger Bannister's four-minute mile as examples. In *Countdown* language, they're both a 'safe 7'. So we'll choose a different one. Let's gamble with a 'risky 9'.

Here's a paradigm shift applied to a current problem. In the UK, ill people are struggling to get doctors' appointments. Doctors' surgeries tend to be open 8 till 5. Basically, to suit the doctors. So, if you're poorly out of hours or, heaven forbid, at weekends, you'll die. The government keeps asking, rather too politely, for surgeries to open longer hours and the doctors keep saying, slightly less politely, up yours.

I like the Japanese model. In Japan, your doctor's job is to keep you healthy. You pay every month if you're healthy and you don't pay if you're sick! I think this simple paradigm shift would get UK doctors' surgeries open on Saturdays, Sundays and late nights. You might even get 24-hour, drive-through surgeries because it would be in the doc's interest to get you fit and well asap! Same problem. *New thinking*.

So here's a bit of a paradigm shift for the world of personal development. Maybe self-improvement is a waste of time.

Maybe *self-remembering* is where it's at.

We fall into a routine. We take things for granted. We stop taking risks. We sink into being comfortable. We settle for mediocrity. But what if the solution isn't to learn a whole load of new stuff but, instead, just peel back a few layers to reveal the good stuff that's already inside?

Welcome to your reminder!

'You cannot be anything you want to be – but you can be a lot more of who you already are.'

Tom Rath

It might sound a little righteous, but this book is for your heart of hearts, for the voice inside your head and for the person you want to be. But, more than anything, it's for the person you already are. It is a reminder that you are already brilliant, *sometimes.* And that you need to start being brilliant *a bit more often*. This book is about reminding you to surround yourself with those who refill your reserves of energy, love and gratitude. Not the miserable bastards who deplete you.

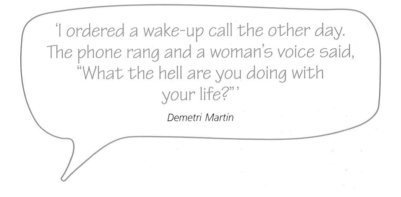

'I ordered a wake-up call the other day. The phone rang and a woman's voice said, "What the hell are you doing with your life?"'

Demetri Martin

May I finish this section with a lovely story, embellished and exaggerated ever so slightly, but pretty much true. We will often sneak these 'silly stories' into the book, partly because they're not so silly and partly because, without exception, they have a lovely meaning.

We'd like to think this book is a wake-up call, so we thought it would be appropriate to share this little beauty – a story about the *ultimate* wake-up call.[1]

---

[1] *Borrowed and embellished from Sir John Jones.*

A few years ago, I was working in South Africa and was put up in a nice hotel in Durban. I wasn't jet-lagged, merely knackered. My mobile phone battery was low and I didn't have my charger, so I was saving its juice to call home. I booked an early-morning wake-up call, explaining to the desk that 7.00am would be fine.

06.45am – phone rang. I thrashed around in the dark and picked it up, not quite sure what to expect. It was a smiley man with a black voice. 'Good morning Mr Andrew Cope. If I may be so bold as to call you Mr Andrew?'

'Morning,' I grunted. 'Who is this?'

'Robin, sir. This is your early-morning call, Robin-style sir.'

'Err, thanks Robin.' But he wasn't finished.

'You requested 7 o'clock Mr Andrew. But it's only 6.45. And that is because we have a wonderful South African breakfast waiting for you sir. I figured you'd need a little extra time to enjoy it.'

'Thanks Robin. That's, err, very kind,' I offered, now more than half awake.

'And, Mr Andrew, you need to know that it's a chilly morning today so please wear a sweater. I wouldn't want you catching a chill and taking it back to dear old Eeengland.'

'No,' I chuckled, 'that'd never do.' And he still wasn't finished.

'So, before I go, are there any taxis you need me to book or any arrangements I can help you with this morning Mr Andrew?'

I was sitting up and smiling. 'No thanks Robin. And you can call me Andy. I'll see you downstairs in a few minutes.'

'Excellent Mr Andy. And I know you're going to have a fabulous day.' I could hear him grinning down the phone.

I had a Cheshire Cat look about me as I leapt into the shower, got dressed and skipped downstairs. I sought out Robin at reception. *Nope.* Concierge? *Nope.* And then I heard him, outside, '*. . . and I hope you have a fabulous day.*'

Robin was the bell boy. His job was to meet, greet and carry cases. He also did wake-up calls. In hotel terms he was on the lowest rung of the corporate ladder.

And I've never met a happier man.

A THOROUGHLY MODERN MASLOW

'For three days after death, hair and fingernails continue to grow but phone calls taper off.'

Johnny Carson

Jenny's 'to do' list for the day

The emotional spectrum runs from depression at the dark end to exuberance at the other. Think Eeyore and Tigger. And, like most spectrums, there are various shades of emotion in between. Most people live somewhere in the middle. They're 'fine'.

'Fine' is synonymous with 'average'. And 'average' is, by definition, what most people are. And, to coin a phrase I use in my school workshops, it's easy to be yourself, *averagely*. It always amazes me how much trouble folks go to attending to their clothes and hair. They polish their shoes. They apply their make-up just so. And then they walk around with a face like a bulldog caught in a swarm of killer bees.

The reality is that life can be rather hard work. We get ground down by 'busyness'. In fact, the word 'busyness' has not only crept into the dictionary, it's also crept centre stage in your life to the point of becoming a standard greeting:

'How are you Andy?'
'Oh, you know, keeping busy.'

It's not just the UK. 'Busyness' has crept insidiously into the developed world. There are so many examples. My son plays 'Kwik Cricket', which, as well as teaching him how to mis-spell the great game, has also shortened it to half an hour.

There was a guy on a course recently and he had four mobile phones on the desk in front of him. *Four!* Just so you know, he had two ears just like the rest of us. He was fixated by his mobile phones all day.[2] At break time he had a special 'technology belt' that he put them in. Andy W nicknamed him the 'John Wayne

[2] *I was thinking what you're thinking . . . drug dealer.*

of modern communications', lighting up like a Christmas tree as his BlackBerry, iPhone and whatever else vied for his attention. BlackBerrys are nicknamed 'CrackBerrys' for a reason!

I delivered some training in London recently. Canary Wharf. *Get me!* That involved a trip on the docklands railway or the 'DLR' as us Canary Wharfers like to call it. For the rest of you, it's an extension of the underground that goes overground! I arrived at St Panc tube, stood for half an hour working out where all the coloured lines went and worked out that I needed the yellow one. Rather proudly, I used the self-service ticket machine (*get me, again!*) and I followed the yellow signs, descending into the Victorian underground to await my carriage. I was idling track-side when there was a tannoy announcement along the lines of 'please accept our humble apologies but there's a severe delay on the yellow line'. The regular London crowd went berserk. This 'severe delay' was causing them some severe stress. As you will have gathered, I'm from out of town so I approached a guy with a London Underground uniform and asked him how long the delay was. He looked ashen faced, delivering the news as though one of my relatives had died. 'Seven minutes sir. I'm so sorry.' He was choked with emotion.

Look here, dear reader, we seem to have reached the point in our evolution when a seven-minute delay causes gnashing of teeth and frothing mouths. For context, I'm from a village seven miles from Derby. If the bus is 'severely delayed' that means you won't be going to town until a week on Tuesday!

This book is an interruption to your busyness. And, yes, we know you haven't got time to to read it! And we know you're skimming it to the point that you missed that there were two 'tos' in the previous sentence.

Robert Holden calls modern life 'the daily blur'. We wake up, hit the autopilot button and the semi-hypnotic world passes us by. We're locked into a routine. And while autopilot helps you get through your day, it doesn't always help you maximise the enjoyment of your day.

Robert proffers some really cool activities. For example, on your happiness scale of 1–10, what would have to happen for you to raise one notch? And then one more notch? In this scenario you'll probably find that happiness is dependent on things that will happen to you in the future.

But if you reword the activity, thus: 'What would have to happen for me to feel better right now?' you might well find that there's a whirring of the cogs *within*. This question often points to changes you can make, in your thinking and attitudes, that will get you a better result.

Some people are so busy that they've erased themselves from their lives. Your routine is more important than you! I spoke about the busyness epidemic at a conference recently and an exasperated, non-ironic voice shouted from the audience, '*I haven't got time to slow down!*'

And that's our point, exactly! Busyness has got a grip of us to the point that we're not immersed in life, we're skimming the surface of it. At work, most people no longer have a 'job for life', just a 'job for the life of the project'. That leaves a permanent undercurrent of uncertainty. There will be a re-structure coming soon. Or, even worse, business is now so footloose that you could be closed down and outsourced to China. Work is squeezing you. Guaranteed, your boss will be saying 'Here are more tasks. We're not taking any of the old ones away, but we'd like you to do these fresh ones too.' *Nice one!*

And, of course, it's not just work. Twitter forces you to squeeze everything into 140 characters. BBC3 has the 'One-minute news'. I recently caught a cookery programme where, in a delicious twist of irony, the winner got their meal immortalised as a microwave dinner. #WTF?

Here's Maslow's seminal 'hierarchy of needs' revamped for the new world. Yes, yes, I appreciate it's an academic gag, but it makes a very good point.

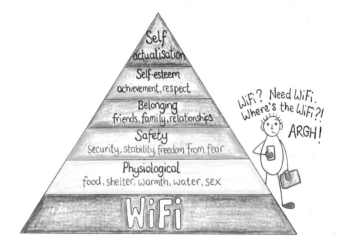

For too many people, modern life has become a dash. A race to the finish line, hurtling through life as if your thumb was pressed on fast forward. And, let's be clear, Andy and I aren't immune. I was stuck in a convoy of slow-moving cars the other day. And I mean *slooooow*. We were being held up by an elderly driver going way below 30mph. I had my family in the car and we had places to go, people to see and things to do.

I started chuntering. 'They're doing it on purpose. Just to annoy me!' I looked in the rear-view mirror. 'There's a massive queue,' I hissed. 'Old people shouldn't be allowed on the road.' We came to a standstill and I couldn't take it any more. I opened the window and shouted, 'For heaven's sake. Get a bloody move on!' And my family started getting annoyed with me. 'Dad, please shut up. You're ruining grandma's funeral procession.'

Scott Adams's clever take on ancient philosophy, '*I get email, therefore I am*', is a good summation of modernity.

The result? Jamie Smart argues that our mental clarity is under attack. Smartphones, hyperlinks, emails from your bed and ticker-tape news are eating our attention like a drunken man eating a kebab (that's hungrily and without caring whether it's good or not). We get mental congestion. Or is it mental indigestion? Or mental constipation? They all seem to fit! And, whichever way, the feeling is the same as the man with the kebab – bloated, lethargic and unsatisfied.

> '*I've got more important things to think about. I've got a yogurt to finish, the expiry date is today.*'
>
> Scotland football manager, Gordon Strachan

The modern world is damaging our health. Last year there were 50 million prescriptions written for people who need chemical assistance to feel normal. And despite being better connected than ever, there are an awful lot of people feeling isolated and alone.

You've almost certainly heard of Attention Deficit Hyperactivity Disorder, probably by its shortened name ADHD. This is a neurological disorder that has a strong genetic component. If you're a teacher, you've most certainly experienced the constant struggle to maintain the attention of children who are easily distracted. Recent research has found a growing number of adults with no neurological disorder who are driven to behave in ADHD-like ways. Maureen Gaffney describes it as 'experiencing an inner frenzy of distractability, impatience, difficulty in setting priorities, staying focused and managing time.'

Edward Hallowell calls it ADT – Attention Deficit Trait. It's not a disorder, as such. It's a cluttered head caused by overdosing on information. Basically, we're becoming self-inflicted stress-heads.

Check this out for another modern disorder. There's something called 'vibrating thigh syndrome' – the feeling that your phone is buzzing when, in fact, it isn't. You keep checking your pocket because you can feel the phantom vibration. And, even more salient, I read a report that says doctors are seeing more and more people who are suffering from 'toasted thigh syndrome' – burning of the skin caused by having a laptop sat on your knee all day. True, I promise.

Single tasking is an anachronism. Even men are having to multi-task (albeit badly, in most instances). My new Kindle has pretty much killed reading for pleasure. It now allows me to access emails and the web, so the magic of reading is thwarted by the opportunity ('for just a second') to check on email or an incoming text message.

And the problem with skimming the surface is that you experience a great deal but, as Robert said earlier, it's a blur. You miss the hidden depths.

Ask yourself, are the best authors the ones who can write a book the quickest? Are the best chefs those who can knock up a meal the fastest? Are the best artists the ones who can paint the quickest? Are the best lovers . . . ?

Apparently, life doesn't always have to be about speed!

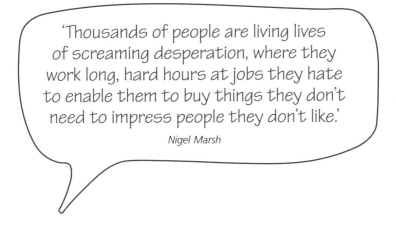

'Thousands of people are living lives of screaming desperation, where they work long, hard hours at jobs they hate to enable them to buy things they don't need to impress people they don't like.'

Nigel Marsh

Please indulge me and allow one more example of 'busyness'. It's my pet subject and is actually a massive impediment to modern-day happiness and wellbeing, so it's worth hammering the point. I did some work at one of the major supermarkets and they told me that sales of oranges are down by 30% in the last five years. The reason? *We haven't got time to peel them.* We're so busy that we'd rather get scurvy than peel a piece of fruit. But grated cheese, ready meals and, get this, pre-peeled hard-boiled eggs are all on the up. The wonderful capitalist world is finding ways of accommodating our 'busyness'. If you haven't got time to stick your eggs in a pan and boil them for ten minutes, we'll provide that service for you.

Now, of course, none of this is wrong. I'm not asking that we harp back to the 'good old days' where there were three TV channels and we actually had time to get bored. I'm arguing that the hectic pace of life is, for the most part, normal.

> 'My grandfather is always saying that in the old days people could leave their back doors open. Which is probably why his submarine sank.'
>
> *Milton Jones*

But if 'busyness' has conned you into thinking working half a day means quitting at 4pm, then it's time for a re-think. If you get impatient as your laptop boots up, you need help. If it's not only the battery on your mobile phone that's drained and you're exhausted by the thought of spending time with your own kids, things are worse than we thought.

Are you sitting comfortably? Then consider this lovely story about the three bears . . .

Baby Bear goes downstairs and sits in his small chair at the table. He looks into his small bowl. It is empty. 'Who's been eating my porridge?' he squeaks.

Daddy Bear arrives at the big table and sits in his big chair. He looks into his big bowl and it is also empty. 'Who's been eating my porridge?' he roars.

Mummy Bear pokes her head through the serving hatch from the kitchen and yells, 'For God's sake, how many times do I have to go through this with you idiots? It was Mummy Bear who got up first. It was Mummy Bear who woke everyone in the house. It was Mummy Bear who made the coffee. It was Mummy Bear who unloaded the dishwasher from last night and put everything away. It was Mummy Bear who swept the floor in the kitchen. It was Mummy Bear who went out in the cold early morning air to fetch the newspaper and croissants. It was Mummy Bear who set the damned table.'

Baby Bear's bottom lip is now trembling but she continues, 'It was Mummy Bear who walked the bloody dog, cleaned the cat's litter tray, gave them their food and refilled their water. And now that you've decided to drag your sorry bear-arses downstairs and grace Mummy Bear with your grumpy presence, listen carefully, because I'm only going to say this once . . .

I HAVEN'T MADE THE F****** PORRIDGE YET!'

I love the pertinence of this familiar story. I especially like it because it makes the very important point that even brilliant people are allowed to lose their rag. Let's look at what being brilliant isn't. Being 'brilliant' *isn't* about always being right or nicey-nicey. And it's certainly not about being walked all over. It's not about sticking an inane grin on your face and pretending to be happy when you're seriously hacked off. Sometimes it's perfectly OK to be angry and upset. Just not all the time!

And, hopefully, if this message has sunk in with Daddy and Baby Bears, you might just make Mummy Bear's porridge in future.

We can't cure your busyness. It's just the way the modern world happens to be.

This book is like hitting 'Ctrl Alt Delete'. Let's have a bit of a re-boot and start afresh. Because, thinking aloud, the chances are that you are living life fast. But are you living it well?

BONUS (TRUE) STORY

Busking

Washington, DC metro station on a cold January morning. A man with a violin was busking. He played six classical pieces for about 45 minutes. He was being filmed and, during that time, approximately 2000 people went through the station, most of them on their way to work.

After three minutes, a middle-aged man noticed there was a musician playing. He slowed his pace and stopped for a few seconds and then hurried on by.

Four minutes later, the violinist received his first dollar – a woman threw the money in the hat and, without stopping, continued to walk.

Six minutes in, a young man leaned against the wall to listen to him, then looked at his watch and started to walk again, presumably with a train to catch.

After 10 minutes, a 3-year-old boy stopped but his mother tugged him along hurriedly. The child stopped to look at the violinist again, but the mother pushed hard and the child continued to walk, turning his head all the time. This action was repeated by several other children. Every parent, without exception, forced their children to move on quickly.

Forty-five minutes later, the musician had played continuously. Only six people stopped and listened for a short while. About 20 gave money but continued to walk at their normal pace. The man collected a total of $32.

He finished playing and silence took over. No one noticed. No one applauded, nor was there any recognition.

None of the commuters knew, but the violinist was Joshua Bell, one of the greatest musicians of our generation. He played one of the most intricate pieces ever written, with a Stradivarius violin worth $3.5 million. Two days before Joshua Bell sold out a theatre in Boston where the seats averaged $100.

This is a true story. Joshua Bell playing incognito in the metro station was organised by the *Washington Post* as part of a social experiment about perception, taste and people's priorities. The questions raised: In a common place environment at an inappropriate hour, do we perceive beauty? Do we stop to appreciate it? Do we recognise talent in an unexpected context?

One possible conclusion reached from this experiment could be this: If we do not have a moment to stop and listen to one of the best musicians in the world, playing some of the finest music ever written, with one of the most beautiful instruments ever made . . . how many other things are we missing?

WIRED FOR STRUGGLE?

'So I got home and the phone was ringing. I picked it up and said, "Who's speaking please?" And a voice said, "You are."'

Tim Vine

Alice was pooped.
She realised that by the time she had
recovered from yesterday then prepared
for tomorrow, there wasn't a lot
left of today

According to my esteemed co-author, we're all born perfect. But, of course, in the interests of generating some debate, I totally disagree. We're born completely and utterly flawed. You pop out into the world and someone slaps your backside. *Nice welcome!*[3] You open your lungs and the starting pistol of life signals that you're off. . .

You are you. You just don't know it yet! And, eventually, you get used to being you. You work out what works and doesn't work for you. You suss the system.

Now I don't want to get too deep too quickly, but have you ever stopped to consider which bit is 'you'?

Is it the body bit? Grab your ear lobe and feel the smoothness of it. The little hairs. That's a bit of 'you', right? Or bite your lip. *Ouch*, that's definitely 'you'. Pull your hair. That's attached, so that's 'you' too. So there's a physical 'you'. That version of 'you' that's basically a bunch of trillions of cells stuck together. And the physical 'you' is very important.

But this book is less about the 'you' that you see when you stand naked in front of the mirror. Yes, yes, we know there are a load of lumps, bumps and imperfections. But herein lies the clue to you #2. Who's the one *noticing* your reflection? Who's the one saying, 'Best suck your belly in mate'? Who's the one *imagining* how good you'd look if you actually put some effort into getting fit?

We reckon this is the *real* you. The lumpy, visible bunch of cells is just the mechanism you use to transport yourself around. The one in your head is the most important. The one that feels

---

[3] *I'm reliably informed that when Andy W was born, the doctor slapped his mum.*

and connects. Some call it your spirit, or personality or inner voice. Steve Peters calls it your inner chimp, that little voice in your head.

If I ask you, 'Do you talk to yourself'? The *real* you is the one who says, 'I don't know, do I?' And that's the version of 'you' that we want to engage. The one inside. Because if we can get through to the *real* you, our job is done.

> 'Auditions are being held to be your best self. Apply within.'
>
> *Anon*

Which, of course, is all well and good but the real you gets hidden. It's not just 'busyness' that gets in the way. We get mummified beneath layers and layers of learning and messages about who we *should* be. There are several versions of 'you' in there. There's the 'work' you. And the 'parent' you. And the 'partner' you and the 'in the pub with your mates' you. Then there's the 'on your own with your inner thoughts' you. It all gets rather complex.

What screws most people up is the view inside their head of how life's supposed to be!

So let's simplify things.

I spend a lot of time loitering outside schools. *No, no, no. Not like that.* As well as delivering 'The Art of Being Brilliant', I also moonlight as a world-famous[4] children's author. That means I get to visit loads of primary schools.

I always choose to park around the corner, and walk. It's awesome. Because as soon as I step out of the car I can hear the buzz. And as I get closer, the noise builds. There's excited screaming as well as peals of squealing, yelling, laughter and unbridled joy. (*Let me add that the excitement's nothing to do with me. It happens every day, in every school, author visit or no author visit.*)

As I arrive at the school gates I sometimes stand and watch. I know, you're not supposed to do that kind of thing in the modern era, but I do. The energy and excitement generated by 300 kids is something to behold. They're playing, skipping and jumping around. There's always an awful lot of running. And hopscotch is alive and well. I have to say, it's a joy.

Cut to the next day. I also deliver 'The Art of Being Brilliant' in businesses, so I'm suited and booted for a high-powered meeting. It feels all corporate and professional. There's no screaming or excitement. Nobody's ever invited me to play hopscotch. There's hardly any skipping and, if I'm being honest, very little unbridled joy.

Children (particularly of primary school age) are a wonderful example of our natural state of being. Their default setting is playful, delirious, curious, fun, joyful and excitable. They're a powder keg of excitement, just waiting to explode.

So what happened? At what point did we become dull, boring and negative? At what point did we stop jumping in puddles?

---

[4] *A child once asked me, 'What's it like to be world famous?', so I must be, all right?*

Can you pinpoint the exact moment when hopscotch became a bad idea?

I doubt you can nail the exact moment. The tap of delirium tends to get turned off gradually, so you hardly notice the decline. And if you're not careful, the gushing excitement of life eventually becomes a drip . . . drip . . . drip. For some people the joy seems to have been turned off completely and their tap has rusted up.

Maybe it's 'life'. Maybe it's 'responsibility'. Or 'stress' or 'routine' or the 'dullness' that life can become. But here's a thought. Could it be that we're happy, positive and curious by default, but somehow we just . . . *forget?*

Because if we revisit the primary school kids, delve a little deeper and ask them, 'What do you want to be when you grow up?' there's more unbridled enthusiasm, often bordering on blind optimism. Astronauts, footballers and actresses are still very popular. I have to say, an increasingly popular female profession is 'nail technician'.

But I have a sneaking suspicion that we're asking the wrong question. Instead of, 'What do you want to be when you grow up?' (bearing in mind many adults still don't know!), maybe a better question is, 'What *kind* of person do you want to be when you grow up?'

That one always throws up some interesting answers. Because this book is less about your occupation and much more to do with your outlook. If you're dead set on being a nail technician, we want to raise your aspirations. We want you to be the happiest, most positive and best nail technician *in the world*. In

39

which case, almost by accident, you'll end up owning and running a chain of beauty salons and be fabulously successful.

Most people have ended up in their current job pretty much by accident. There are very few primary school kids who dream of being a 'housing officer' or a 'sales executive' or a 'teaching assistant'. But they're the kind of jobs that we end up doing.

In short, it's not what you do that concerns us so much as the manner in which you do it. Bob the Builder provides a classic example of the inner-superhero that I'm talking about. He's an ordinary guy in an ordinary job. Bob's been to the same college as all the other builders and has got the same NVQ3 in bricklaying. It isn't the job Bob does that is extraordinary, it is the attitude he brings with him. And, dare I venture, it is Bob's attitude that makes him the best builder in the world.[5]

And that's the kind of difference we hope to make. I guarantee that all the nurses and obstetricians who delivered the royal baby will be showered with OBEs and knighthoods, while the thousands of 'ordinary' nurses just keep turning up and getting on with it. Single parents don't get medals of honour or invited to the Queen's garden parties. They just get on with it.

Ordinary folks, like you and me, we just keep plodding along. Ordinary 'everydayness'[6] makes up a massive proportion of your life. So, let's enliven the 'ordinary' and give your everydayness an extraordinary tinge.

---

[5] Yes, I have a Bob the Builder poster in my office. Right next to the tennis girl with no pants on!
[6] We will occasionally make words up, simply because they feel right.

Bonus Activity

Imagine you are 119 years old and have one minute left before you die. Your great-great grandchild is holding your hand and says, 'Before you die, tell me what I should do with my life.'

What would you say?

MADONNA, QUEEN AND THE FAT LAD

'Cinderella is proof that shoes can change your life.'

Anon

All Jean wanted was a little more
than she would ever get

Madonna was, famously, a material girl, living in a material world. And, as life gets faster, we tend to seek solace in 'things'.

Governments design systems and go about it in different ways, but ultimately it all seems to be about cash. In the same way that Harry Potter can be summed up as 'boy wizard fights arch enemy at boarding school', politics can be summed up thus: Right-leaning political parties seem to be about smaller taxes – keep a bit more of what you earn and incentivise everyone to try and earn something. Leftism, by contrast, is about bigger government. Tax those who can afford to pay a bit more and redistribute it to the less well off.

But, beneath the surface, the message is the same: 'Vote for us and we'll make you a bit richer'. The right wing parties want to make the rich a bit richer. The left wingers want to make the poor less poor.

The Western free-market philosophy seems to be about creating desires. Every advert on the telly is designed to make you unhappy with what you've currently got, thereby persuading you to part with your hard-earned cash. Or, if you haven't got any cash, the banks will persuade you to borrow some. If you're already in debt, the payday loan companies will happily oblige.

The underlying philosophy, so ingrained that we often don't realise it's there, is 'you will fulfil your desires by spending money'. We have coined a phrase, 'retail therapy', which translates as 'I'll be happy so long as I'm in Westfield'.

We seek good feelings in shopping or food. We are seduced into wanting the latest thing – cool jeans, designer labels, a new TV, Sky, faster broadband – that'll make us happy.

Oliver James calls it 'affluenza' – '*a painful, contagious, socially transmitted condition of overload, debt, anxiety and waste resulting from the dogged pursuit of more.*' My daughter's caught it. She buys clothes like they're going out of fashion!

The Eastern philosophy is interesting. Summing up a bit like the Harry Potter example, it is more about letting go of the desires. On just about every level it seems like a much simpler model. Enjoy being alive. Live in the moment. Be aware. Be happy *NOW*. And part of being happy NOW is about letting go of the desires.

And intellectually we know that *almost* makes sense. I have a car. And I know I should be happy with my car. Because it's a good car. But there are other cars out there that are, quite frankly, much better than my car. And while I don't covet my neighbour's wife, I wouldn't half like his motor!

I came across a great word the other day; 'Musterbation'. It is defined as '*the elevation of things we'd like to have into things we believe we must have*'.

And, the chances are, you are a musterbator. I know I am. Andy W most definitely is.

I've got a degree in Economics and I remember learning about the difference between 'wants' and 'needs' and how people applied rational principles to satisfy them. But the whole thing comes crashing down like a pack of cards when we apply human *irrationalities* to 'wants' and 'needs'. Common sense tells us that 'needs' are necessities of life. And 'wants' are the 'nice to haves'. But modern marketing means we're bombarded with messages that are turning our 'wants' into 'needs'.

If you ask my son, he doesn't *want* a new mobile phone, he *needs* one. It has somehow been elevated in his psyche to the point of survival. It's up there with 'water' and 'oxygen'. As a 14-year-old male, he is spending an inordinate amount of time in his bedroom, presumably musterbating about getting a new laptop.

My wife saw a pair of Jimmy Choo shoes in a magazine and said, 'I *have* to have them.' Her eyes went all gaga and her voice exorcist deep. There was no 'want' about it. The language sort of implied, 'if I don't get those shoes I will die'.

It seems like Madonna, the material girl, was right. As were Queen. To paraphrase one of their immortal lines, we want it all and we want it NOW!

We're all musterbating like crazy!

People go to extraordinary lengths to feel good. Some seek the meaning of life in the shopping precinct. Or we seek shallow solace in food, or drink. There are 24 beers in a case and 24 hours in a day. *Coincidence?*

Some pray or visit a monastery in India or Mecca. The last place most people look is right under their feet.

Here's a thought that might shake your belief in the 'material girl'. If you list the top 10 happiest moments of your life (go on, we dare you to have a go), there's unlikely to be a single product on there. It'll be experiences. It'll be things you've done – moments of joy and achievements that have left you grinning rather than products you've purchased.

So, although this section has been devoted to Madonna, I'll leave you with Fat Boy Slim. What if the secret to feeling good lies in ourselves, our relationships and experiences? What if it's always been like that?

What if happiness and flourishing are *right here, right now?*

BONUS STORY

Dirty Windows

A young couple moved into a swanky apartment in a new neighbourhood. They sat in their kitchen having breakfast, watching the world go by. The woman saw her neighbour pegging out the washing. 'That laundry's not very clean,' she tutted. 'She either needs a new washing machine or better washing powder.'

Other than crunching on his toast, her husband remained silent.

His wife's comment was exactly the same the next day. And the next. 'Why on Earth is that woman hanging out dirty washing?' she sighed in disgust. 'She needs lessons in basic hygiene!'

And her husband crunched, knowingly.

On the fourth day his wife plonked herself at the breakfast table with a gleeful smile. 'At last,' she said, pointing at their neighbour's washing line. Her husband followed her gaze to the neatly arranged clothes line, where the whites sparkled and the colours shone. 'All of a sudden she seems to have learned to clean properly.'

And her husband broke his silence. 'I got up early this morning and cleaned our windows.'

And so it is with life. We view the world from inside our head. Our eyes are our windows on the world. Before we give any criticism, it might be a good idea to check our state of mind and ask ourselves if we are ready to see the good rather than to be looking for something in the person we are about to judge. It's easy to be critical. It's easy for our windows to become grimy.

So, to stretch the vision metaphor just a little bit too far, we don't want you to go all 'rose tinted'. Not everything in the world is good and bright and fantastic. But, if you follow our advice and view the world through our 'positive-tinted' spectacles, the world's a lot brighter than you think.

YOUR INNER TORTOISE

'The foolish man seeks happiness in the distance;
the wise grows it under his feet.'

James Oppenheim

Beccy decided she couldn't be happy
forever. It was too long. She pencilled it in
for Fridays between 4 and 5, and then
again after 10 on Saturdays

My job takes me out and about.

A few years ago, I began observing people and asking some questions, such as:

- Who is happy?
- And, equally pertinent, how do I know they're happy?
- And, even more pertinent, what can I learn from them that I can apply to my own life, so I can be happy too?

I wandered through my train. The people in the 1st class carriage had comfy seats and somewhere to plug their laptops in, but they didn't look any happier than my lot in pleb class.

I observed people sat next to me in motorway traffic jams. People in big, posh cars didn't look any happier than those in jalopies.

I noticed Nandos was full of chatter and the posh restaurants weren't. *Interesting!*

I studied the managers above me. They were higher in the food chain and earning more money than me but they looked exhausted, just like the rest of us.

Curiously, there didn't seem to be any sort of pattern. It was as though really happy people were in a tiny minority, spread across all sections of society.

Plus, after deciding to throw myself into the study of human flourishing, I hit a brick wall pretty much immediately. It seemed nobody could even define 'happiness'. Even the clever boffins couldn't agree.

And there was another issue that cropped up early on. It seems that those who are significantly happier than average tend to stand out, but not always for the right reasons. Is it possible to live as an upbeat, passionate, confident, happy version of yourself without everyone else thinking you're a sanctimonious, cringe-worthy, 24-carat plonker? If you stick a grin on your face and bounce into work on Monday with a war-cry of, *'Don't those weekends drag? Isn't it great to be back at work everybody?'* your colleagues will assume that a village is missing its resident idiot. Wandering around with an inane grin fixed to your chops is, quite frankly, disturbing.

Which is why some of the American gurus grate a little. I know this book is destined to be available in the bookshops of LA and New York, and I don't want to alienate our US readership. I'm not getting at you, guys. This is merely an observation. On this side of the pond we have a cultural thing that we call 'the curse of mediocrity'. I've heard British society described as a 'whingeocracy'. In short, it's in our culture to have a moan. And, if you want to be accepted as 'normal', you have to join in.

Meanwhile, on the other side of the pond, you have Zig Ziglar (rest his soul and all that), one of the greatest and most revered speakers ever. Don't get me wrong, I love Zig. But I remember picking up one of his books and thinking 'what kind of name is that?' And I read the blurb on the back of the book and it transpires Ziggy babe was a Texan, with a holiday home in California. That's 356 days of sunshine. And his holiday home was on the beach, so Zig could throw his patio doors open and listen to the Pacific Ocean pounding in the background. And I turned to page 1 and Zig started by saying, *'I don't have an alarm clock. I have an opportunity clock,'* and it was like someone scratching their fingernails down a blackboard.

No Zig. It's not like that here! My nearest seaside is Skegness and, I promise you, the beach is quite different from what you're used to.[7] When I open my curtains in the morning, it's not

---

[7] *Sorry Skeg, a cheap gag.*

California. In the immortal words of Frankie Boyle, it's like a holding pen for a Jeremy Kyle show.[8]

So, although we hope to appeal to a global audience, we have both feet firmly planted on these shores. As a Brit recently pointed out, somewhat optimistically, *'There is an "i" in happiness and a "we" in wellbeing.'*

Only to be stamped down with a rather droll reminder, 'There's also an "i" in miserable and three in pessimistic!'

I'm going to defer to one of my new-found heroes of personal development, Nigel Marsh. You'll see his quotes popping up a few times. Nigel's a Brit who deems it acceptable to emigrate to Australia, but despite that, I highly recommend his books. They're about personal development and happiness without you really noticing, which I think is very clever indeed. I'm also going to quote him directly because there's a naughty word coming up and it seems slightly less caustic if *he* says it rather than me. Nigel talks about what he calls 'post traumatic success syndrome' whereby you've achieved marvellous things in your life, yet you still feel shit (that's not the naughty word, there's a much worse one coming . . .).

'No external victory is ever going to satiate the self-esteem monster. It's a hungry fucker. You don't need to feed it, you need to slay it. To feel better, it's a waste of time trying to change my external world. I have to work on the inside not the outside. It's about changing my perspective and attitude – not just about achieving more.'

Nigel Marsh

---

[8] *Andy W tells me that Mansfield hasn't got a twin town. It's got a suicide pact with Scunthorpe.*

This short paragraph is the best summation of the modern end of personal development that I've ever read. I've long given up trying to change or 'improve' other people. I've given up blaming the government or my manager or the weather for me feeling grouchy. I've stopped blaming fast-food restaurants or my 'lifestyle' for making me fat. And I no longer curse the rush hour for giving me an ulcer.

I lay so comfortably on the bed of excuses that I think I nodded off. I was lying there, luxuriating in blame, waiting for my life to improve and, before I knew it, a couple of decades had whizzed by. But that doesn't matter because I'm like you, I have the rest of my life to find happiness. But then a thought struck me, what if it takes longer than that?

So, wearily at first, I poked my toe out from beneath the duvet of inertia. Which actually gives you a big clue about our collective view on 'positive thinking'. We're not big believers you see, unless it's backed by positive action. You can't just *wish* to be upbeat and positive. You have to make things happen. Some delegates like the idea of the theory bit, but we know that when the going gets tough (as it always does, remember the self-esteem monster and 'busyness' from a few minutes ago?), they slip back into default bog-standard, 'do what I've always done' mode.

Of course, no matter how positive and upbeat you are, you'll still get negative thoughts popping into your head, because that's how thoughts work. We are programmed to respond to external stimuli.

Human beings are wired to be able to experience a whole gamut of emotions, including those that would be classed as 'negative' – anger, jealousy, rage, terror, sadness and the like. I

55

really don't think we should be *denying* them. Negative emotions aren't all bad. We feel them for a reason!

Fear, for example, is useful. *Sometimes.* You don't go walking down dark alleyways at night for a reason. Similarly, fear stops you walking too close to a cliff edge.

The problem arises when we magnify negative emotions and use them against ourselves.

Fear stops you walking off cliffs but it also stops you presenting at a meeting.

Shyness stops you making an idiot of yourself but it also stops you meeting your perfect partner.

Pessimism protects you from disappointment but also hampers your happiness.

I'll explain why we're wired for doom and gloom in a later chapter. For now, believe me when I tell you that your default position, unless you choose otherwise, is likely to be negative.

LIFT OFF

'Our instinct is to externalize the forces that are holding us back, but, in fact, that's not the problem, is it?'

Seth Godin

 You may now....

....update your Facebook status

Time is the ultimate scarce resource, which makes 'time management' such a fascinating concept. Contrary to popular belief, you cannot *buy* time, all you can do is displace it from somewhere else. There are 1040 minutes in a day, day in, day out. One of the most important aspects of 'time management' is not how to manage it, but how to eke out the best *experience* you can in the limited time you have available to you.

How do you spend it? There can be a tendency towards inertia and reality TV. Things that you know will do you good take a little effort to get into.

When a rocket pulls away from the launch pad, it uses 90% of its fuel in the initial 'getting going' phase. And humans work on a similar principle. The energy involved in getting off your backside and engaging in something meaningful seems significant. The fact that, once engaged in said activity, you come alive and feel invigorated, is easily forgotten.

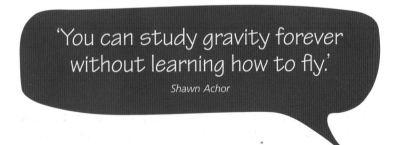

'You can study gravity forever without learning how to fly.'

Shawn Achor

So, this book is partly about breaking the chains of inertia. In our previous book we majored on how the choice to be positive is one of the most significant things you will ever do. Choosing to be positive is simple, *but not easy*. We sometimes describe it as common sense but not common practice.

We've already spoken about human beings being anything but rational. Here are some more things that are *common sense but not common practice*. Our irrationality gets in the way:

- **Stopping smoking.** The vast majority of smokers accept that it's bad for their health and that they are paying a massive amount of money to, effectively, hasten their death. And it's not like being killed by The Goodies! It's going to be one of those scary, 'clogged lungs so you can't breathe' deaths. I mean, logically, why would you? Common sense tells you to stop. But I'm told there are plenty of young people keen to take up the habit.
- **Reduce your drinking.** Ditto, except the death will be with a bulbous red nose.
- **Stop watching rubbish TV.** We know we shouldn't, but it's on, so we do.
- **Get more exercise.** We know we should, but we don't!
- **Get eight hours' sleep.** Everyone knows that optimal functioning happens after a good night's kip. But few people get enough sleep.
- **Eat healthier.** Five a day and all that. Freshly cooked; sit down as a family. We know it makes perfect sense, and yet we end up grabbing some fast food or a microwave meal.
- **Spend more time with the kids.** This is a biggy. We know we should, but it's all rather exhausting.

All the above fall into the 'common sense but not common practice' category. And all are simple but not easy. Exactly like being your brilliant self on a consistent basis.

Positive habits are like a financial investment. Do them now, and regularly, and they'll give you automatic returns later. Habits are simply things that we do repeatedly. Your brain is elastic. Scientists call this 'neuroplasticity'. This means your brain is a marvellous piece of kit that is always learning and changing.

Often, at the habit-forming stage, willpower is not enough. Let's take regular exercise as an example. It's a battle. There's hassle involved. Rather than fighting the habit, we believe you must change the habit. And that involves changing the underlying thinking.

We know we want more out of life than TV and Facebook. I got sick to death of getting out of things because I couldn't be bothered. Shawn Achor calls it the path of least resistance. We call it laziness! That's why we end up sitting in front of the TV, vegging out on fast-food meals.

- It's easier to watch TV than write your novel.
- It's easier to stay in bed for an extra half hour than get up and exercise.
- It's easier to moan about the weather than stick your wellies on and go jump in some puddles.
- It's easier to watch a talent show on TV than learn to play the guitar.
- It's easier to watch Jamie Oliver and then go and buy a ready meal than cook your own.

Basically, we're inherently lazy buggers, drawn to things that are easy and convenient. And, unfortunately, being self-critical and sinking into negative conversations is easier than shining brightly.

We're trying to 'make ourselves' happy and positive. As we intuitively know, and will prove in subsequent chapters, there is effort involved in being your best self. But what if less effort was the key? Less *trying* to be happier and more *allowing* yourself to be happier.

Mmm. Ponder that one for a wee while. I'll come back to it later.

LESS PAIN,
MORE GAIN

'God will not look you over for medals, degrees
or diplomas, but for scars.'

Elbert Hubbard

Rhonda wondered why there was never
enough happiness to go round but it was
amazing how far trouble could stretch

Here's something interesting.

First the pleasure bit. Your body is calibrated in such a way that it can predict exactly, in space, where your limbs are. That's why you can hit a tennis ball when you're on the run. If you think about it, that's an amazing feat of awareness. Your body just seems to know where the racket needs to be at a specific moment in time to hit the ball with the right force in the right direction.

Sorry, I said that was interesting. I lied. This is the interesting bit . . . what that means is that you can't tickle yourself. Your brain is so good at sensing where your fingers are that the elements of surprise and randomness (both essential prerequisites for that perfect tickle) are eliminated.

But schizophrenics can tickle themselves. And, without pushing 'positive thinking' to its absolute limits, that's one hell of an upside!

For the rest of us, David Eagleman goes to great lengths to explain how to tickle yourself in his magnificent book, *Incognito*. In case you're interested, it involves attaching a feather to a time-controlled joystick. Sounds like a faff, and possibly a bit kinky.

Now to the pain bit.

Diets. There are thousands of them. And quite a few entice you in with the '*maximum weight loss, minimum effort*' mantra. I don't want to wee on anyone's camp fire here, but the only way to lose weight is to burn up more calories than you take in. I always think the dieting ads should be honest, maybe with a disclaimer – '*Weight loss involves a lot of actually being really effing hungry.*'

Similarly, in terms of 'self-help', people read books or listen to audios and often find it difficult to put into practice what the books suggest (because their own habits are working against them). The result is that nothing really changes.

We promised to immerse you in the shallow end of academia, so consider this the footbath on the way out of the changing rooms and into the pool area.

The source of your brilliance is already inside you! So, *phew*, the search is over. You can stop looking. Life's been a massive game of blind man's bluff. You've been going round and round in circles, then fumbling in the dark, stumbling, groping and hitting your shins on the coffee table of life. *Getting warmer, warmer, almost there . . . no, colder. Much colder.*

Take off the blindfold. Stop spinning. Look where you're going. Search inside yourself. This is true 'self-help'.

You are a walking powder keg of potential change. You can change at any moment. *Boom!* You can change your knickers. You can change your bed. You can change your football team (*I sooo wish that were true*). You can change your brand of yoghurt. You can change your job. You can change your mind, your mood or your habits. I readily acknowledge that some of these changes are easier than others.

It's comforting to know that your brilliant self is always inside you, sort of bubbling under the surface. It gets covered over with stuff we *think* we know. We accumulate layers. We learn how to be. We want to fit in and be 'normal' so we do what everyone else does. That's the game folks.

I've learned that if I walk into a business meeting and drop my trousers, that's generally not acceptable. It's not how we play the game. So, for the most part, I try not to do it and I'm trying to get Andy W to stop it too.

On a more mundane level, I've learned that if someone asks me, 'How are you?' I'm *supposed* to answer, 'Not too bad, considering.' Or, 'I'll be all right at 5 o-clock'. Both are pitched at just the right amount of acceptable drollness. If I said, 'Bloody awful. I'm thinking of going to jump off a bridge later,' that's too negative and would arouse interest.

At the other end of the spectrum, 'I feel so awesome I could burst with enthusiasm,' will simply piss people off. So I've learned to conform.

Human beings are made up of a cocktail of emotions, often shaken *and* stirred! Bad ones are in the mix too. And they seem to rise to the top almost effortlessly. We link these feelings to outside events, often past events, things that have happened to us that have caused us to feel this way.

We need to understand the source of these feelings. Although they are triggered by external events, the actual feelings are created within us. That's a bit spooky. Hang in there, it will become a lot clearer later on. Remember, we're still in the chlorinated footbath of academia. We'll explain more when we get you in the shallow end.

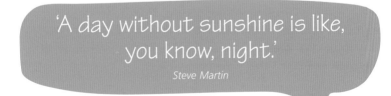

'A day without sunshine is like, you know, night.'

Steve Martin

Another nice analogy is that your brilliant inner self is like the sun behind the clouds. Returning from a lovely sunny holiday, we flew in stunning sunshine until the captain announced we were beginning our descent to East Midlands. We descended through the clouds, into the rain below, skidded to a halt on the sopping wet tarmac and stepped out into a British force 9 gale. But, hang on, it was sunny up there!

The sun is always there. It's just obscured. Just like your inner brilliance.

Now, depending on how far along the self-help road you are, this next sentence can be a bit stressful.

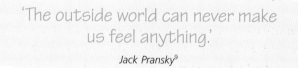

'The outside world can never make us feel anything.'

Jack Pransky[9]

I'm aware that that's a tough one for a lot of people. If you've experienced something awful in your life (and everyone has, frankly), surely you've got every right to feel bad about it? Let's follow Jack a bit deeper into the undergrowth of the self-help jungle.

'When we truly realise everything we experience, our problems, whatever we call "reality" or "the way it is", is really only a product of our thinking, everything changes for us. Our experience of life changes.'

Jack Pransky[10]

---

[9] *See that we included this as a quote to make you angry with Jack rather than us? Clever!*
[10] *Did it again. Quoted Jack to take the heat off me!*

67

Now, here's the truth, the old version of me (the bog-standard, slightly grouchy, sceptical pessimist) would have immediately jumped on the mumbo-jumbo bandwagon and picked massive holes in the philosophy above. 'This Jack bloke seems to be saying that if I have a bad day, it's my fault! Who the fuck is he anyway? He doesn't have to share an office with my boss! He doesn't understand that my manager has slashed the budget and we've got fewer people to do more work. And he doesn't know I have to care for my elderly mum or that I've got massive credit card bills. That's the *reality* Wacko Jacko.'

And I would have let my *thinking* about what Jack said ruin my day. Which, if you're clever enough to still be with me, makes his point exactly!

Thankfully, the new me is a little more open-minded. I want my experience of life to change. I want my experience to be a positive one. I want loving relationships and a fulfilling career. More than anything, in the brief time I have on this Earth, I want to be happy.

What Jack Pransky is really saying is that it's not speaking in front of an audience that's freaking you out. It's your *thoughts* about speaking in front of an audience. It's not the aeroplane flight that stops you from visiting your sister in Australia, it's the *thought* of the aeroplane flight. And, truthfully, it's not the bullying or abuse you experienced as a child, it's the *memory* of it that's robbing your self-confidence.

Your consciousness really has just one priority – to create your reality. Whatever you are thinking and feeling, right now, is created by thoughts which your conscious brain then turns into reality.

> 'Reality is merely an illusion,
> albeit a very persistent one.'
> *Albert Einstein*

Two things immediately spring to mind. Firstly (and rather confusingly) your reality isn't real. And secondly, you must recognise it's not anyone else's reality.

I know you can probably feel one of your headaches coming on, but please bear with me. This is important.

Let's give you an example. If someone cuts you up in the traffic, your thoughts become aggressive, manifesting in anger and your consciousness makes it 'real'. So you chase them across town.

Now, we're not saying that the other driver wasn't in the wrong or that s/he didn't exist, we're dipping your toe into the shallow end here by suggesting the event is neutral. What determines your experience of being cut up is your own thinking.

We concur with Jack Pransky on many levels. If you delve a bit deeper, the message is that we get in our own way. We are the ones stopping ourselves from feeling great! And that's quite invigorating because, if we follow the logic, we don't have to work on anyone else. Just ourselves. And that's do-able.

So, before we move on and look at a bit of science, let's ponder one of the most common questions we are asked on our workshops: 'How do we change other people?'

I used to flounder a bit on that one, maybe offering some withering and faltering advice. The truth is that I don't really know. But I think the answer is above. It might well be that we can't change other people.

I mean, technically, in advanced 'brilliant' mode, you can create environments where others are also in a position to have the same level of thinking that you have, but that's a black belt in self-help. For now, relax in the notion that we don't need to change other people.

This is all about you. Once you've mastered this stuff, their annoying habits will no longer be annoying.

INDIANA JONES, THE THERAPIST

'When his life was ruined, his family killed, his farm destroyed, Job knelt down on the ground and yelled up to the heavens, "Why God? Why me?" and the thundering voice of God answered, "There's just something about you that pisses me off."'

Stephen King, Storm of the Century

There's effort involved in changing. This chapter is about the paradigm shift of making *less* effort. Once you realise that all the good feelings you've ever experienced are already inside you, you're immediately looking in the right place and you have to work less hard to access them.

I will once again defer to the awesome Jack Pransky, who says holding a beach ball under water is an effort. Letting it go, allowing it to burst to the surface, isn't work at all. Translate that! What if *stopping* yourself being brilliant is hard work? Suppressing all that energy and vigour and positivity! Why would you? *Whoosh!* Let that beach ball go!

Traditional therapy tries to figure out what your problems are. It's been the same since Sigmund Freud's day. Traditional psychotherapy isn't designed to create flourishing. It's designed to curtail misery. It's about fixing people so they're able to function normally. A central theme of Freud's work was that happiness is an illusion. The best we can ever hope for is to keep our misery and suffering to a minimum.

So, as the client, you are *supposed* to bring all your problems to the session. It's an archaeological dig into your issues. That's how it works. That's how it's always been. And your therapist encourages you to talk about your shit, dredging it up, re-living it.

'So, Mrs Williamson, tell me about when you first met the Radio One DJ.'

Therapy was, and to some extent still is, about digging deeper into our problems. We end up ruminating on them. I think that's what cows do when they chew the cud. They digest things three times.

'*And can you recall the first time you visited him on* Top of the Pops?'

As a football fan, there's hardly a Saturday goes by without a minute's silence for an anniversary of something bad. England played Brazil and there was a combined minute's silence. It was something like the 40th anniversary of the Munich air disaster, the 20th anniversary of Bobby Moore's death and a tragedy in a Brazilian nightclub where people were burned to death. I'm not belittling any of those events. They were dreadful. But after pondering them for a full 60 seconds, I felt awful. And I wasn't even at any of them!

'I'm in therapy at the moment. I don't need it, obviously, but I got all these psychiatrist gift vouchers for Christmas which my family clubbed together for. What I wanted was a crossbow.'

Sean Lock

Let's just, for a moment, apply a bit of common sense. Let's assume you've had a bit of a gardening accident and gone and stuck a fork through your foot. *Ouch.* That'll be a trip to casualty, a four-hour wait, a few bandages and a tetanus jab.

Do you go poking it with a stick to heal it? I'm fairly sure you won't open the wound up every night, re-playing your mishap, getting the prong inserted just like it was the first time you had your accident. No, you leave the bloody thing alone and it heals from within.

I can hear the whole of the clinical psychology industry railing at us. '*It's not right. It's not that simple. You don't understand clinical practice.*' I (vividly!) remember doing a session for some counsellors and therapists at one of the London Universities and my talk went down like a fart in a spacesuit. They'd trained for a decade to discuss problems, tracing them back to source, ruminating on all the bad things in life. And here was me talking glibly about happiness and flourishing. I pointed them to the very funny Bob Lockart 'Stop it' sketch (YouTube it, it's brill) and they tied me to a horse and ran me out of town.

A GROUNDHOG LIFE?

Natasha had a ticket for the good life
but could never find the entrance

Groundhog Day, what a great movie. Even if you haven't seen it you'll be familiar with the phrase. As a delegate once said, slouching into a training session, '*Same shit, different day.*'

And he's kind of right. Life can become a little bit . . . samey. I call it 'having a C+ life'. Everything's just kind of 'OK'. In school report terms you 'could do better'.

I noticed on the news that there's a town in Scotland called Dull. It was on the news because it's recently been twinned with a town in America . . . called Boring.

And, metaphorically, life can become a bit like that. The alarm goes off at the same time every day and you hit the snooze button. You have a time slot in the bathroom. You sit at the breakfast table, in the same seat, eating the same cereal/toast with same milk/spread, listening to the same radio station, drinking from your favourite mug. You drive to the same place of work, mix with the same people, get home and watch the same TV programmes.

You get the point. I've lost track of the number of people I've researched who, when the alarm goes off at stupid o'clock, have a feeling in the pit of their stomach that says, 'I can't do this any more. I certainly can't do it for another 20 years!'

It isn't a great way to start the day and is a world away from Zig Ziglar's 'opportunity clock'.

> On being left in a parking lot for 500 million years . . .
>
> 'The first ten million years were the worst,' said Marvin, 'and the second ten million years, they were the worst too. The third ten million years I didn't enjoy at all. After that I went into a bit of a decline.'
>
> *Marvin the paranoid android, Douglas Adams,* The Restaurant at the End of the Universe

Too many people are simply ground down by the relentless pace of life.

I have a theory that in 500 years when they look back on 'Elizabethan 2.0' (or E2.0 as we'll surely be known), they'll marvel at what we went through. The whole explosion of technology, the rise and rise of the internet and social networking, the banking crisis, Arab Spring, crippling European recession, globalisation, multiculturalism, gay marriage, Clinton, Obama, Blair, Cowell . . .

The morbid obesity of change is sitting square on my chest. *I can't breathe!*

We feel great sporadically but most people have their eye on the weekend or a holiday in a wishing-their-life-away sleepwalk. But here's a painful truth – life is the culmination of the little things in your life. And it's these little things that make the big thing that is your life. I don't think life is always about making one momentous decision (although, in some cases it can be), it's much more about making lots of small but brilliant decisions.

You might need to brace yourself for this next bit. It's probably best to sit down or, if you're reading this on the Tube, hold on to the person next to you. I've already suggested that most people I know (me included) are driven by 'busyness'. Even children are manic nowadays – their days, weekends and evenings crowded out by social and electronic media.

So here's a controversial thought . . . What if our frantic days are really just a hedge against emptiness?

What if our 'busyness' serves as a kind of existential reassurance – obviously your life cannot possibly be silly, trivial or meaningless if you are so ridiculously busy, completely booked up and in demand every hour of the day.

I can't help but wonder whether all this histrionic exhaustion isn't a way of covering up the fact that most of what we do *doesn't actually matter.* I'm not having a dig at you, I'm merely trying to provoke a thought. And if I am accidentally having a dig, I'm having a dig at me too!

What if we've become superb at masquerading as 'busy' to paper over the cracks of meaninglessness? I think this is, at the very least, an interesting thought and, at the very best, an earth-shattering realisation. Please ponder it for a while and I'll come back to it later when I'm feeling brave enough.

I'd like to conclude this section with another fairly major thought. It's probably rare that you do nothing. I mean 'nothing' as in an idleness definition. Not reading or watching telly or on your iPad. Absolutely diddly-squat, bugger-all lazy nothingness. I would suggest idleness is not an indulgence or a vice; it is as indispensable to the brain as sunshine is to your happiness.

I think doctors should be prescribing a period of bone idleness. The space and quiet that idleness provides are necessary conditions for standing back from life and seeing it whole; for making unexpected connections and waiting for the sudden strike of inspiration.

Think about Archimedes's 'Eureka!' moment in the bath. Or Newton sitting under a tree when the apple fell on his head.

But, of course, we haven't got time to stop and ponder.

Exactly!

HAPPINESS
TERRORISTS

'I went to the doctor and he said, "You've got hypochondria." I said, "Not that as well!"'

Tim Vine

If Rhianna was going to become old and embittered, she needed to get some practice in

We get asked all the time, 'What do you do for a living?'

In the olden days, when Andy W was trying to impress a young lady, he would lie. He started with little fibs like 'tree surgeon', graduating to 'fighter pilot' and, if he really wanted to impress, his all-time favourite, 'dolphin trainer'.

He's got an entire back story about how he used to work with a dolphin called Rocky at Morecambe MarineLand. '*I loved Rocky so much and we did everything together when I was younger,*' he says, sniffing a nostalgic tear away as he tells me how one day he just had to release Rocky into the wild. '*It was the right thing to do.*'

I remind him that he's actually recounting the story of *Free Willy*, that Rocky didn't ever exist and that when I met him he was working as a waitress in a cocktail bar.

Nowadays he doesn't need outright lies, he just stretches the truth. If you ask Andy what he does, he's an internationally renowned best-selling self-help author. Which provokes the next question, 'Are your books all about positive thinking?'

Andy W says he used to reply yes, 'but now I'm not so sure because some people have given positive thinking a bad name; they take it too far, and I want to punch them in the face! And that's not positive thinking, is it?'

He mulls over another example of when his positive-thinking halo slipped. 'I picked a colleague up once to take them to work and as soon as he got in the car he turned to me and grinned, "Andy I've already decided we are going to have a brilliant day." I think he had read a Brian Tracy book. I knocked his front teeth out. Well, I didn't but I thought about it, again not very positive thinking.'

So it's got to be worth exploring why this happens. Why do even the most positive people have negative thoughts?

Have you noticed how most people spend a great deal of time moaning? It's seems to be our national pastime. We grumble about the weather, the economy, the 'yoof of today', work, traffic . . . pretty much anything is fair game.

We don't want to upset any of our loyal readers, but here's a gentle nudge – in 30 years, when you look back at today, these are the 'good old days'!

Guy Browning talks about what he calls the 'four horsemen of negativity': *Boredom, Sameness, Drizzle and Tiredness*.

Individually, they cause minor glumness. And collectively they lead to what he calls '*irritable bastard syndrome*'. And, let's face it, it's an easy set of cards to hold.

If you play this hand regularly, you will be what we call a 'mood hoover', which is meant in a descriptive and fun manner. Mood hoovers do a lot of huffing and puffing, rolling of eyes and tutting, and we call them 'mood hoovers' because they're expert at sucking all the life out of you, leaving you feeling rubbish as well.

> 'Some cause happiness wherever they go; others whenever they go.'
> Oscar Wilde

Latterly I've started describing them as a bit like Darth Vader – lots of heavy breathing and they inhabit the dark side. And, let's be honest, we can all sink into being a mood hoover. How many of you are in the habit of getting home from work and moaning about how bad your day's been?

I shared an office with a mood hoover once and she'd wander in at the start of the working week, rolling her eyes, 'Monday morning, it's tragic. Here today, here tomorrow.'

Controversially, we think slipping into the mood hoover zone is acceptable . . . so long as you don't live there!

I remember delivering 'The Art of Being Brilliant' to some 15-year-olds in Leicester and a six-foot, brick shit-house alpha male stood up, raised his hand and said, 'Sir, I've just realised. I come from a long line of mood hoovers. My granddad's one. My dad's one. My sister's one.' He stopped for a second, seemingly stunned by the revelation. 'I think my dog might be one. And, do you know what sir? They've passed it down to me.'

And that lad's pretty much nailed it. The first few years of your life are what Morris Massey calls 'The Imprint Period'. Essentially, this is a very impressionable early phase when you pick up habits of thinking and behaving. His parents have indeed *inadvertently* taught him to be negative. They didn't teach him in the sense of sitting him down and instructing him to be negative, he just copied what they did.

When you speak to hard-core mood hoovers, you get heavy eyelids very quickly. I think, as we continue to evolve, positive people might evolve to have ear lids as well. As a sort of inoculation against having the life sucked out of you by mood hoovers' incessant moaning.

> 'My capacity for happiness,' he added, 'you could fit into a matchbox without taking out the matches first.'
>
> *Marvin the paranoid android, Douglas Adams,* The Hitch-hiker's Guide to the Galaxy

Yet, bizarrely, it seems to me that often those who really and truly have grounds to moan, don't.

I don't want to do a David Brent, but can I take an example of a Paralympic athlete or, closer to home, Andy W's dad?

Here are a couple of Andy W's favourite things his dad says and does.

Scenario 1: The Hospital

Recently, Andy's dad went to the doctors and they suspected there might be something seriously wrong with him. He was sent for a full medical, blood tests, bone scan, the works. Obviously, Andy W was very concerned. So after ordering himself a new black suit (just in case) he phoned his dad to find out how long he had left.

'Did you get your results from the hospital, dad?' he asked.

'Yes, there is nothing wrong with me son. The consultant said I'm as fit on the inside as I was when I was 21 years old.'

85

With a happy tear in his eye, Andy replied, 'That's brilliant news dad, you must be over the moon.'

'Well,' he said in a dreary tone, pausing for effect, 'I have to go back in five years and who knows what will be wrong with me then.'

'Some people find fault like there is a reward for it.'

Zig Ziglar

Scenario 2: Eating Out

Andy's dad: 'What you having?'

Andy: 'Steak.'

Andy's dad: 'Why?'

Andy: 'Because I just fancy it.'

Andy's dad: 'I don't know what I fancy.'

Andy: 'Oh, erm, can I help in any way?' (Big mistake asking if he could help.)

Andy's dad: 'What will your steak be like?'

Andy [slightly exasperated]: 'Who do you think I am Dad? Mystic Meg? I can't see into the future. I'm guessing it'll be a slab of meat. With some chips.'

Andy's dad: 'Don't get smart lad. Right, I'm having fish.'

The food arrives.

Andy's dad: 'Your steak looks amazing. I wish I'd had steak instead of this fish. I suppose I will have to eat this fish now?'

Andy: 'Would you like to swap dad? I'll have your fish and you have my steak.'

Andy's dad [shaking his head]: 'Seriously son, how do you expect me to eat steak with my teeth?'

I'll leave Andy W to explain . . .

'I don't want to paint the wrong picture of my dad because, as far as being positive is concerned, he has achieved some amazing things. When he was 27 years old he was diagnosed with polio and spent four months in a coma, during which he lost 10 stone in weight (you don't get results like that at Weight Watchers). My dad lost the use of his left arm and the muscles in his neck. He's got a 50p-sized hole in his neck where the tracheotomy didn't heal. He's approaching 80 years old and, because of the loose muscles in his neck, his head is beginning to lean noticeably to one side. (As I always tell him though, "It could be worse dad, at least you don't carry it around under your arm." He is so lucky to have a happiness expert as a son.)

My dad has an amazing life story that he never mentions. Imagine being struck down in the prime of your life, going into a coma as a fit 27-year-old man with a wife and a 2-year-old daughter, coming out four months later paralysed down one side, weighing four stone, with a hole in your neck.

We have all had rough nights out, but I've never experienced anything like that!

However, growing up I didn't even know my dad was disabled. It never occurred to me. He always worked full time and did everything any other dad did. The only thing I did notice is the fact he was the only dad I knew who could blow cigarette smoke through a hole in his neck.

The reason I tell you all this is that my dad is definitely a mood hoover. He loves moaning about anything and everything. His moaning is a habit. But, unlike some other mood hoovers, he really has got something to moan about.'

Andy's dad doesn't moan about big stuff. And we're allowed to speak about him in this book because his moaning is good-natured. We don't think there's anything wrong with having a bit of a grumble, if it's funny. Or if it's genuinely warranted.

We readily acknowledge that it's not *The Waltons* out there folks! But often our whinging isn't amusing or warranted, merely habitual and wearing. There's a mood hoover mate of mine[11] whom I bumped into at a school fete. It was a gala fund-raising event and, as always, the grand finale was the raffle draw. 'I never win,' he boasted. And, sure enough, ticket after ticket was drawn and he proudly kept showing me his. 'Not even had one of my colour. Not even close.'

And then, with an announcement of 'Blue 883', he won. Just like that! Cue a big cheer and slap on the back from me, as he shook his head and stumbled towards the stage. There was a

---

[11] *Let's just analyse that sentence before we go any further. Mood hoovers can be perfectly good friends. They're not horrible people, just stuck a little on the dark side.*

rapturous round of applause and he chose his prize before sheepishly walking back to our table, a very small smile of surprise illuminating his face. He showed us his bottle of wine. 'All the good prizes were gone.'

He'd done it again. He'd pulled another defeat from the jaws of victory.

You will recognise these traits in the people you know. Maybe even in yourself.

And I'm not saying it's wrong. It's normal.

We're picking these out as semi-humorous examples of low-level, everyday negativity. The problem is that this is just the tip of the iceberg. Negative self-talk can rob you of energy and confidence and put the boot into your happiness. Quite honestly, it can get to the point where it is anything but funny.

A BALANCING ACT

'There is nothing in a caterpillar that tells you
it's going to be a butterfly.'

Buckmeister Fuller

Tom was the kind of guy who stopped
the microwave at 1 second just to feel
like a bomb defuser

The chances are that if you've ever been on holiday you've looked places up on Trip Advisor. For the uninitiated, it's a website that allows tourists to review their holidays. There are millions upon millions of hotel reviews.

And have you noticed that you can't resist checking the 1-star ratings? There might be 273 5-star reviews, but you're drawn to the one miserable rating when someone found a pubic hair on the toilet seat. You've discounted the awesome service, poolside bar, free cocktails, chocolate on your pillow and the sea view. This miserable reviewer has deleted all the wonderful things that happened on their holiday to the point whereby the only thing they can remember is the pubic hair! Why would you want to take their advice?

Tip: Cheer yourself up at the next funeral you go to by hiding a tenner in your black suit today.

Now, once again, in the interests of balance, I'm not suggesting that a pubic hair on the toilet seat is good news. I wouldn't go out of my way to request one. Neither do I particularly crave loo roll that's folded into a point. I mean, that's not how I leave it at home for the next person. And I'm not fussed about having a chocolate on my pillow. And, quite frankly if I had a fridge in my bedroom that was stocked with midnight nibbles, I'd be the size of a small bungalow.

Imagine a set of scales. On one side we're going to load on the 273 bits of good news from Trip Advisor: excellent pool, free cocktails, awesome service, world-class breakfasts, comfy bed, well-appointed room, sea view, etc. And on the other side of the scales my wife states that we can't go there '*Because it has a pubic hair*'. The principle of negativity, the fact that in evolutionary terms, bad weighs more than good, means that one single hair can weigh more than all the good stuff. In the real world, that's why one snotty customer can ruin your day. Or, if you're a teacher, one naughty child can ruin your class. Or all the traffic lights being on red on your way to work can ruin your journey.[12]

In the interests of exploring the science, we'll have a look at why later. Why are we programmed to give that one negative more credence than the avalanche of positives?

But, before we can get there, we need to have a cursory glance at our pet subject, positive psychology.

Positive psychology is often passed off as 'popular psychology' or a bit 'new age', largely by those who haven't actually studied it.

It's a relatively new field of study and, I promise you, it's heady stuff. It doesn't aim to denigrate traditional strands of psychology, nor supersede them. But it does recognise itself as being radically different. Rather than viewing psychology purely as a treatment for the maligned, it looks at the conditions necessary for human flourishing.

Psychology has traditionally been interested in where people's lives have gone wrong, and what has resulted because of it. And it's been a worthy field of study for hundreds of years because psychology has been about helping people recover from ailments. The result is that we know an awful lot about anxiety, depression and a whole host of maladies. The pharmaceutical

---

[12] *Or, on a bad day, all of the above.*

industry has blossomed on the back of medication to treat depression and illness. Not to mention the counselling and therapy boom.

However, until relatively recently, happiness, wellbeing and flourishing have been a bit of a mystery. Happy, positive people tend not to be ill, you see. And because they're not ill, we've never studied them.

Positive psychology practitioners have gone off piste and taken to studying happy souls who have a spring in their step and whose lives are positive. Positive psychology remains in its infancy and, yes, it's often subject to criticism. I mean, why study happiness when there's so much misery to cure? And don't we already know how to be happy? 'Happy-ology' . . . isn't that a bit, you know, hippyish?

My answers are:

What if part of the cure for misery was to study and learn from happy people?

And, if we already knew how to be happy, surely there wouldn't be any need to dole out 50 million anti-depressant prescriptions per annum.

And as for it being a bit 'new age', absolutely bang on. *Because this is a new age!* And a new age calls for a shift of thinking.

Positive psychology is undertaken by proper heavyweight academics[13] and it's not far off being a paradigm shift that we mentioned earlier. Psychology has been turned on its head.

---

[13] *Clever ones, not necessarily fat ones.*

Positive *thinking* is merely one tiny strand of positive psychology. Surrounding yourself with a great lifestyle and material goods may seem to lead to happiness, but how you really feel is governed by what goes on inside your head. When you go out of your way to think positively, you actually purge yourself of negative self-talk.

But why do we have negative self-talk in the first place? This is a question we'll sort for you in the next section.

CYNICAL THINKING

'I'm not bad, I'm just drawn that way.'

Jessica Rabbit, from Who Framed Roger Rabbit?

Petunia was too damned busy for
anything important

The Cynics were real people! As were the Stoics, dating back as far as the 5th century BC.[14] So we can safely say that whinging and moaning have been around for a long time!

Let's deal with the Cynics first. For the Cynics, the purpose of life was to live in virtue, in agreement with nature. As reasoning creatures, they thought people could gain happiness by rigorous training and by living in a way which was natural for humans, rejecting all conventional desires for wealth, power, sex and fame. Instead, they were dedicated to leading a life free from all possessions. As a result, Cynics ended up begging on the streets. And, if historical accounts are to be believed, they were quite forceful in criticising those who did have possessions. Cynics wandered around the city very openly chastising people. I guess that's where the modern connotation evolved from.

Cut to the Stoics. Yes, they were real too! The modern connotation of stoicism means you face up to things bravely and calmly, serenely tackling the world's ills with a stiff upper lip. Make some tea and carry on. It's so wonderfully British!

Go back 4000 years and the Stoics were quite a force. Rather than struggling to avoid all thoughts of negativity and potential disasters, the Stoics would actively dwell on them, staring them in the face. William Irvine calls it 'negative visualisation'. Stoics themselves called it the 'premeditation of evils'. It is the belief that by confronting the worst case scenario, you are effectively sapping it of its power.

The result was that Stoics were big believers in fate. I'm probably over-simplifying the Stoic philosophy but, 'Shit happens. But if you *expect* it, it's not so shit!' is probably not a million miles away.

---

[14] *BC, that's 'Before Computers'. OK?*

'Fate is like a strange, unpopular restaurant filled with odd little waiters who bring you things you never asked for and don't always like.'

Lemony Snicket

The Stoics' belief was that happiness achieved by positive thinking could only ever be fleeting and brittle. They believed that to achieve genuine happiness you would have to suppress all the possible permutations of negativity and it wasn't worth the effort. Negative visualisation (*plan for and expect the worst*) would therefore generate a more dependable calm.

If we follow the timeline from BC to AD, we see that early Christian teachings were threaded with messages about how life on Earth was meant to be one of suffering and sacrifice. It wasn't until you entered the Kingdom of God (i.e., that you died) that things would perk up.[15]

And that was how it stayed until the 17th century, a time of 'enlightenment' when, to quote McMahon, '. . . people in the West dared to think of happiness as something more than a divine gift or other worldly reward . . . for the first time in history, comparatively large numbers of people were exposed to

---

[15] *I appreciate that if we major on 'religion' we're immediately on stony ground (nice pun, if I say so myself). So we'll give it a couple of paragraphs, max. However, whatever God you follow, the likelihood is they'll be offering you something pretty spectacular in the afterlife. So, to use an earlier analogy, religion puts happiness somewhere over the rainbow, way up high.*

the novel prospect that they might not have to wait until death. They could, and should, expect happiness as a right of life.'

Holy mackerel! That sounds like a breakthrough. But, nope, not really. The liberating potential of this new creed – the belief that happiness was a natural human condition – entailed an unfortunate corollary. If individuals *ought* to be happy, but weren't, maybe it followed that something was wrong? For centuries, Christianity had justified a sense of suffering, pain and dissatisfaction. It made sense that life was tough. To quote McMahon again, 'The long-term impact of "enlightenment" had precisely the opposite effect, creating pain, guilt and stress as a consequence of failing to be happy.'

Plain, simple English again? We suppressed happiness for thousands of years, saving it until we were six feet under when, arguably, it was too late. And when someone finally said it was OK to be happy, we struggled. Which made us unhappy.

I'm not sure if that's the ultimate irony, extreme Sod's Law or an example of the classic Ellie Roosevelt quote 'you're damned if you do and you're damned if you don't.' But it does seem a mighty waste of people's happiness potential.

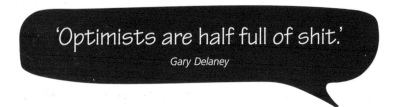

'Optimists are half full of shit.'

Gary Delaney

Modern-day psychologists have invented something called 'Ironic Process Theory', which is a cosmic big-bang of Cynic, Stoic and Sod. This line of study explores how our effort to suppress certain thoughts or behaviours results, ironically, in them becoming more prevalent.

How often do parents say, 'Don't spill your drink,' and the child is so over-cautious about gripping their cup that they forget the dog asleep on the carpet and, five seconds later, we're all wailing over spilt semi-skimmed?

How many golfers have prayed a silent prayer, 'Please not in the water. Please not in the water . . .' Plop!

But, of course, it's difficult *not* to worry. And worrying about stuff uses up mental bandwidth. Famously, Einstein didn't know his own phone number. He carried it around on a piece of paper because he didn't want to clutter his brain. Homer Simpson is the same. He told Marge he wouldn't go to night school because every time he learns something new it pushes some old stuff out of his brain.

Both Einstein and Homer are wrong. Your brain has plenty of capacity. Don't *worry* (there's that word again!) about it filling up. The trick is to fill your brain with the right stuff.

Your brain is often likened to a computer. One comparison we do like is that your brain has a spam filter. It selects the crap and dumps it before it gets to your conscious awareness. Which is fab so long as we trust the spam filter to block out the bad stuff and only allow in the good stuff.

Just for a second, imagine if your computer's spam filter worked in the opposite way and it blocked all the wonderful emails that said what a great job you were doing. Instead it deleted all the good stuff and brought only bad news, stress and misery to your attention.

You're working away when 'ping' (incoming email, and you know you can't resist):

> 'Having trouble with your erections? We sell pills that can help you with that.' *Oh, right. Hey ho, back to work.*

'Ping'.

> 'Feeling lonely? Meet this great woman. She's ever so lonely too.' *Nice one, thanks. That'd give me a chance to use my new pills too!*

Back to work. 'Ping'.

> 'Short of cash?' *Well, yes. How did you know?* 'Guaranteed loans of £10,000. Instant, no questions asked.' *I'd be daft not to! I mean, those pills and that lonely woman might be expensive, right?*

Hey presto! Your reverse spam filter will have brought all your sexual problems, loneliness and money worries to your attention. *Hello loser!*

And your brain is a bit like that too. Far too many people have the good stuff filtered out and a brain that brings screaming negatives to their attention.

Spam filters will only block what they're programmed to find. So will your brain. So the 64-megabyte question is, what have you programmed?

MEET THE
ANCESTORS

'You can't indulge in blue sky thinking when the clouds
are thundering and the rain is torrential.'

Richard Gerver

Philomena had worked out that life on
earth was expensive but consoled herself
that it did include an annual free trip
around the sun

Catastrophising is in your genes. It's been passed down through the ages, not just by religion and the Cynics, but by everyone.

It's the same with all creatures. Let's take mice as an example. Famously, it's always the second mouse that gets the cheese. The positive, confident, happy-go-lucky mouse was a victim of its own enthusiasm and never got round to passing its genes on! The bar on the mouse trap comes down with one hell of a thwack.

In a similar fashion, it's your most cautious ancestors that survived. If we open our minds and go with Darwin's theory,[16] we're descended from creatures that roamed during the Ice Age.[17]

We had positive and happy ancestors who, when the sun peeped out, thought, '*Ooh, nice sunny day. And I bet it's going to be nice again tomorrow. Let's have a bit of a celebratory do.*' And they got crushed by the ice.

Those who survived were cautious. '*It's a nice day today so I'll work extra hard in case it's not nice again tomorrow.*' So, for the happy ones who partied like there was no tomorrow, there *was* no tomorrow. The cautious ones stored some food. Hence, it was their genes that passed down.

To us!

> 'She got her looks from her father.
> He's a plastic surgeon.'
>
> *Groucho Marx*

---

[16] *Other theories are available.*
[17] *If you've seen the movies, Andy W is descended from Sid the sloth.*

Your brain has evolved by seeking out and attending to potential threats. Worrying is the brain's default position. It's sometimes referred to as 'psychic entropy'. Basically, as the pubic hair anecdote has already proved, a negative emotion has the ability to trump a positive emotion every time.

Steven Pinker notes that most of this goes on at a subconscious level. For instance, have you ever wondered why it feels great to climb a hill and observe a lovely 360° view? It's because, deep in our psyche, there's a feeling of security. You can see all the way to the horizon so are able to spot enemies who might be advancing – and that gives you a nice feeling. We also instinctively like big trees, rivers and lakes – not just because they provide shelter and food, but because they help us identify where we are.

Conversely, we don't like dense jungle and darkness because our vision is obscured and danger could be lurking. We are also programmed to dislike things that are bad for us – snakes, rats, bitter tastes, the smell of rotting food, the sight of blood and politicians.

Our radar is honed in on bad news, which is why so many people worship at the altar of negativity. The weather is too hot or too cold or too *something*. In the UK we are great at having inquests into things that have gone wrong. At any point in time there are three or four going on. Inquests into why hospitals are killing people or why schools are failing. They are presided over by an ex-judge who spends five years investigating what's gone wrong and produces a 5000-page report with 455 recommendations that nobody reads. I'm not sure it's uniquely British, but it's a good example of our proclivity to study negativity.

The technical term for it is 'negativity bias' and you experience it every day. Negative events and bad feedback are more influential and have a longer-lasting impact than positive stuff.

Here are some examples:

- Apparently, it takes 25 acts of life-saving heroism to make up for one murder.
- In relationships, it takes five good deeds to make up for one bad one.[18]
- You're more likely to remember losing a bet than winning one.

And here's a classic example for anyone who's ever got a speeding ticket. How many times have you broken the speed

---

[18] I know what you're thinking guys . . . only five?

limit and *not* been caught? And not been bothered that you haven't been caught? I'm guessing at thousands of times. You haven't rushed through the door in a state of great excitement, hyperventilating and fist pumping while you regale the tale of speeding at 85mph all the way down the M6. 'And then, guess what, I even went 45 in a 30! And still I didn't get caught. Awesome!'

And the one time you do get caught? There's plenty of cussing and frothing at the mouth. 'Haven't the police got better things to do? Bastards! Shouldn't they be catching real criminals?'

The one negative sure weighs heavy.

But why? As explored above, in evolutionary terms, ignoring negativity would be life threatening. We learn to pay attention to potential danger. We're tuned in so it's what we see, hear and feel because it saves our skin. If you ignore danger, you're a gonner. Whereas if you ignore a positive, you're still alive. That's how we become socialised from infancy.

Therefore (and this is crucial), a negative mind-set is likely to be your default position, unless you apply intentional strategies.

Can I just share one more example, taken from real life? And, guys, it might just save your marriage. If you give someone a compliment or criticism, which do you think they're going to remember the longest? Yes, 'negativity bias', explained above, means people will hold on to the criticism.

I am dragged to the shops once a year on a husband and wife spree. There's usually some sort of do coming up and Louise needs a new dress, so I'm hauled along for a second opinion. I do what all dutiful males do – I sit patiently while Louise bashes around in the M&S changing room, until eventually, the curtain swishes back and she's standing there. 'Ta da! What do you think?'

Now I could take one look, shake my head and say, 'Deffo not. It makes your bum look big and I can see your muffin tops. To be honest Lou, that dress makes you look like a sack of potatoes.'

Assuming my marriage could withstand that sentence, I know (and you know) that the curtain would swish shut and we would shop in stony silence from then on. The cool atmosphere would last at least a week and my infamous 'sack of potatoes' comment would be thrown back at me until the day I died.

So, what if I'd taken a different approach? What if, as the curtain swished open, I'd stood gawping at my beautiful wife, eyes agog. 'Holy shit, you look stunning. I lurve that dress. The colour, the shape, everything. Whoever designed it had you in mind.'

My wife would look at me suspiciously. 'You're just saying that. I'm sure it makes my bum look big. You're just trying to get this over with aren't you? Is there some football on or something?'

The law of 'negativity bias' means the criticism will sink into my wife's bone marrow, never to be forgotten or forgiven. But the compliment bounces off her, like Batfink's wings of steel.

> 'Women don't want to hear what you think. Women want to hear what they think – in a deeper voice.'
>
> *Bill Cosby*

So here's a magic number for you . . . 2.9013. Make sure you jot it down.

In positive psychology land this is called the *Losada Line* and it's the ratio of positive to negative comments necessary to create flourishing relationships. In plain, simple English, it takes about three positives to make up for one negative. Dip below the Losada Line and working/family relations will suffer.

In fact, 2.9013 is the *minimum* ratio required to keep relationships bubbling. Marriages that dip below the magic 3:1 ratio are very likely to end up in the divorce courts.

A positivity ratio of 6:1 is ideal. In my research, I call it 'flourishing'.

Anything over 12:1 becomes a bit sickly and too nicey-nicey. Something I alluded to earlier – if you overdo the positivity you will make people feel queasy. Vomit-inducing Von-Trapp-style 'singing while you're being pursued by the Nazis' is perhaps a step too far.

Plus, and I think this is a point that is often overlooked in other personal development books, please note the '1' in the ratio. The Losada Line *isn't* 3:0, which means that some negativity, criticism and pessimism is fine. If someone's had a dreadful haircut (a 'scarecut') you don't have to lie. 'I see you've had your ears lowered' or 'Do you want me to get the bastard that did it?' will sometimes suffice.

You need to be in the real world folks. Just re-positioned toward the upper end of the positivity and optimism spectrum.

THE INVENTION
OF HAPPINESS

'The problem with the gene pool is that there
is no lifeguard.'

Anonymous

Blodwyn would definitely start
living soon....
....but not today

So, if we're programmed to be negative, cautious and pessimistic, why on Earth was happiness invented?

I love Barbara Fredrickson's model of 'broaden and build' because, at last, there's an academic argument that explains the evolutionary significance of happiness. It seems that positive emotion works in exactly the same way that negativity doesn't.

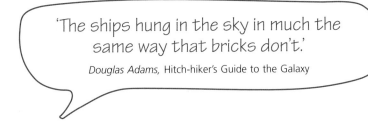

'The ships hung in the sky in much the same way that bricks don't.'

Douglas Adams, Hitch-hiker's Guide to the Galaxy

Negative emotions close down your thinking. Danger, for example, narrows down your choices to just two: 'fight' or 'flight'.

Fredrickson argues that the experience of positive emotions opens the mind and enhances our choices. Positivity enhances creativity. Positive emotions fuel enthusiasm, innovation, optimism and drive. They enhance our ability to take in information, increase our capacity for intellectual complexity and our ability to explore alternatives.

Positive emotions generate what Kim Cameron calls 'upward spirals' towards optimal functioning. *Phew!* As well as enabling us to feel good in the now, it seems there might be a valid evolutionary role for happiness and positivity after all.

So, if your ancestors were sitting around in the cold, tearing at pieces of raw meat but managing to feel good about their day's hunting, their minds would open up to possibilities about the future. 'Hey,' says your great-great (to the power of 500) grandpa, 'I've got an idea. What do you reckon would happen if I rubbed these two sticks together?'

And, whoosh, McDonalds is born!

> 'Give a man a fire and he's warm for a day, but set fire to him and he's warm for the rest of his life.'
>
> Terry Pratchett, Jingo

And, once again, this kind of fits with your own experience. When you're feeling down, the world closes in and you can't think of a way out. That's essentially the feeling of depression; locked into negativity, trapped in a world of self-pity, with seemingly no way out.

When you're upbeat, your brain fires off with all sorts of creative solutions. Just about anything's possible.

The big question we want to grapple with is, how? How do we get into a state where our brain is firing and energy zinging? Nobody's ever got to the bottom of this before because they haven't studied deeply enough. Brace yourself, because in the next chapter we're immersing you in the grey goo of quantum mechanics.

QUANTUM PHYSICS FOR DUMMIES

'Thought creates the world and then says,
"I didn't do it!"'

David Bohm, quantum physicist

Time spent eating an orange:
- ■ Peeling
- ☐ Picking off stringy bits
- ■ Actually eating the orange

Professor Cortex had finally worked out why sales
of oranges were on the decline

Quantum physics! You might be best getting yourself a cup of black coffee (or something stronger!) but please come straight back.

It's Andy W here folks. I'm in charge of this chapter, so brace yourself for a bumpy ride. Brain in gear? Here we go . . .

One of the immutable laws of physics is that energy can be neither created nor destroyed. Not many self-help books question the laws of the universe, but if you've sat through some of the meetings I've sat through, you'll know that physics has got it wrong, energy can be completely destroyed.

So folks, we're about to question the laws of quantum mechanics. Andy C introduced some of the Jack Pransky stuff earlier and suggested it was the equivalent of stepping through the chlorinated footbath of academia. Well, goggles on and get your budgie smugglers adjusted. We're jumping in!

Here's how it started. I was having lunch with my co-author, Dr Cope, and after finishing a mouthful of burger he looked up at me and announced, 'I want you to write a chapter for the new book.'

'Cool,' I said, excited but worried at the same time. I'm keen as mustard but getting sentences out in the right order isn't my forte. And I don't want to big him up too much, but he's published dozens of books and has sold a million copies. And I'm from Mansfield. And here he was, trusting me with a whole chapter. I tried to play it cool. And, of course, I always pride myself on being positive. 'No problemo gaffer,' I fibbed. 'What do you want me to write about?'

'Quantum physics.' He said it so matter-of-factly, like you would if you noticed the weather was clouding over.

It was a few minutes before the waiter stopped hitting me hard on the back and the mouthful of burger was dislodged from my windpipe. My eyes were watering. I glugged some water and spoke in that husky voice that is reserved for those near-choking moments, 'Did you say, "quantum physics"?'

Andy C nodded. I think he'd enjoyed my near-death experience. 'We've got Brian Cox and Stephen Whatsisface, with the electronic voice,' he beamed.

'Stephen *Hawking*,' I wheezed, almost Stephen Hawking-like, still struggling with food in the wrong pipe. 'The world-renowned expert in quantum physics. Who's studied quantum physics all his life to the point of becoming a professor of it. That *Whatsisface*?'

'He's the rascal,' beamed Andy. 'Except I want it Andy Whittaker style.'

So that got me thinking. How hard can it be to write a chapter about the most complex subject known to humankind? On the bright side, I have read *The Holographic Universe* by Michael Talbot and been on some heavy-duty NLP courses, so here goes . . .

'Anyone who is not shocked by quantum theory has not understood it.'

Niels Bohr

If you're a proper quantum physicist, you're probably best to look away now. For everyone else, if it's OK with you I'm going to avoid quarks, string theory and the Copenhagen question. In fact, I'm going to mix and match a few subjects and invent a new concept. I'm calling it 'Quantum Psychology'. Let's start with the basics.

If you're of a certain age, you'll remember an old BT advert when Maureen Lipman phoned her grandson to see how he'd done in his exams. It was all rather bleak until he announced he'd got an O-level in Sociology. And she was chuffed to bits. 'You've got an "ology".'

That puts psychology up there with all the other 'ologies'. Some people argue that psychology is not a proper science. Not like physics. Or chemistry, with its unfathomable periodic table.

Oh no, dear reader, psychology is much harder than that. Physics has immutable rules and laws. Particles are totally predictable. They always do the same thing. Heat them up and they get excited and jostle around a bit. Exert a force and off they trundle in a totally predictable direction and with calculable velocity.

Imagine how hard physics would be if particles could think and feel? That's the territory we're in. The 'laws' I'm about to describe are a bit more fluid.

'Red sky at night, light of shorter wavelengths being dissipated through water vapour and atmospheric dust.
Red sky in the morning, same.
Not as catchy as the original but a lot more accurate.'

Tim Vine

It's a bit like a cross between *The Matrix* and *The Bible*. Nothing exists outside of you. You are the centre of the universe. There is only you. Your entire external experience, the world in which you exist on a daily basis, isn't actually real.

There, I've said it!

As Andy C alluded to earlier, the world you're experiencing is a direct reflection of what's happening inside you, in your nervous system, so any issues you have in life are *inside* you, not *outside* you.

If your head is still on, I will endeavour to explain, firstly in an academic way and then in a way a lad from Mansfield would.

One of the central 'problems' of quantum physics is to calculate the energy levels of a system (that system could be you). The energy operator, called the Hamiltonian (abbreviated to H) gives you the total energy. Finding the energy levels of a system breaks down to finding the eigenvalues of the problem. Like this:

$$H|\psi\rangle = E|\psi\rangle$$

The eigenvalues can be found by solving this simple equation:

$$\det \begin{vmatrix} H_{11} - E & H_{12} & H_{13} & H_{14} & \dots \\ H_{21} & H_{22} - E & H_{23} & H_{24} & \dots \\ H_{31} & H_{32} & H_{33} - E & H_{34} & \dots \\ H_{41} & H_{42} & H_{43} & H_{44} - E & \dots \end{vmatrix} = 0$$

$$H\psi(r) = \frac{-h^2}{2m}\Delta\psi(r) + V(r)\psi(r) = E\psi(r)$$

With me so far?

Of course you're not!

Let's try again, this time like a bloke with a GCSE in Woodwork would.

Fact: in quantum physics your head can blow straight off your shoulders at the speed of a thousand gazelles.

'If you are in a spaceship that is traveling at the speed of light, and you turn on the headlights, does anything happen?'

Steven Wright

So I thought it might be safer to play a game instead. Firstly, for this game you need to believe, or at least suspend your utter disbelief, that nothing exists outside of your nervous system. Remember, though, it's only a game.

Cool. Now, go and get an object. An orange is always good. Or a TV remote control. Hold the object in your hand and take a good look at it. OK, now close your eyes for three seconds. Now, eyes open and *Ta Da!* There it is again! That's all there is to it!

That's quantum physics, albeit simplified a little bit.

The question is, how did you *know* the orange/TV remote control was there (i.e. that it *existed* and was real) while your eyes were closed? You might answer, 'I could feel it, you Muppet.' In which case, let's delve a little deeper into the weird and wonderful world of particles. Let's do the same thing again but imagine your arms were paralysed in a tuna-fishing accident and you have no feeling. So, no sight and no feeling! And your sense of smell is blighted by a terrible primary school incident with some Evostick.

Look at the object. Close your eyes and open them again. How could you prove the object was there when your eyes were closed?

No, no. Stay with me, please. I know there's a desperate desire to skip this bit but hang in there. It's my only bloody chapter!

So, come on Sherlock, how can you prove the object exists? The only things you can have as 'proof' are your thoughts, memories, pictures and smells of the orange, which are *inside* your nervous system.

Now place the object in front of you (or, if you're still playing the tuna-fishing role, hold it in your paralysed arms), close your eyes again for five seconds and answer the question, 'How can I prove it exists (is real)?'

All pretty straightforward so far, I think you'll agree. So, let's ratchet up the level of interest into the Twilight Zone. Hold onto your pants, dear reader, while I explain about Schrödinger's Cat. This is a very famous quantum physics experiment. Basically, you put a cat in a box along with some poison that has a 50/50 chance of killing the cat. You then close the lid and wait a few minutes. You don't know whether the cat is dead or alive until you open the box. The suspense will be killing you (and, to be fair, the poison is probably killing the innocent mog). You, opening the box, decide the cat's fate. The cat is neither dead nor alive until you open the box and prove it one way or the other. One minute you are minding your own business, next minute you look in a box and you're a cat killer!

We wanted to recreate the experiment but didn't want to endanger any cats. We're not monsters! Instead I have got my mate Eric, who is really desperate to get a mention in the book, locked under my stairs with a loaded gun, a torch and a Katie Price novel. I know after reading one of her books Eric has a 50/50 chance of killing himself.

I have to leave Eric there for a few hours. The really exciting part is that I don't know whether Eric is alive or dead until I open the door. Admittedly there were some strange noises coming from under the stairs (I think there might have been pictures in the book) but those noises quickly subsided into silence. Eric is neither dead nor alive until I open the door.

Shazaam! Quantum physics, Mansfield style!

But what do Schrödinger's Cat and Eric's suicide dilemma actually mean in real life?

It's all about 'reality'. If we believe (or at least suspend our disbelief) and accept that nothing exists outside of us, we're half way to cutting through the strangulating undergrowth of the self-help jungle. We create reality through the way we interpret the world. And, with a modicum of practice and a bit of Vulcan mind dexterity, we can learn to create a better reality.

In case you're still struggling (and I know you are!), if we are not happy with the way our world is, then we can change it. It's an inside job. Holy moley! That means happiness is on the inside! But, following the logic, that also means I'm personally responsible for creating the world in which I live. Yikes! That sounds a bit heavy.

Now, of course, it's easier to think of this as a load of hokum. I mean, you've learned that your happiness and positivity depend on external stuff like the weather, right? Or a pay rise. Or what day of the week you're on (Mondays are generally worse than Fridays, at a guess). And if you live in a cramped council flat that's hardly your fault, right? And if you didn't get a pay rise that's your company's fault. And if you haven't got a job, that'll be the government's fault. And if you did poorly at school, that's got to be the teacher's fault, surely.

> 'The trouble is, learning requires re-thinking and re-thinking hurts.'
>
> *Dan Rockwell*

Learning something new requires us to give up some of our old knowledge. To develop a broader vision we must be willing to forsake our narrower vision. It's always more comfortable *not* to do this, to stay where we are. To grow personally and spiritually we need to actively seek new ways of thinking.

A Sioux parable

The creator gathered all of creation and said, 'I want to hide something from humans until they are ready for it. It is the realisation that they create their own reality.'

The eagle said, 'Give it to me. I will take it to the highest mountain.'

The creator said, 'No, one day they will go there and find it.'

The salmon said, 'I will hide it at the bottom of the ocean.'

'No, they will go there too.'

The buffalo said, 'Give it to me. I will bury it on the great plains.'

The creator said, 'No, they will dig deep into the earth and find it there.'

Then grandmother mole, whose sight was poor but insight great, said, 'Put it inside them, for that is the last place they will look.'

The creator said, 'It is done.'

THE UMWELT

'I went on a positive thinking course. It was shit.'

Gary Delaney

Strap yourself in, there's some conceptual stuff coming up. I don't want to get too metaphysical, but, as humans, we are only detecting a tiny slice of the world around us. What we are able to experience is limited by our biology. Take human vision, for example. We have special receptors at the back of our eyes that ping into action when they catch some radiation, and that causes an avalanche of signals to the brain, which creates vision. So, hey presto, your brain filters these signals and you can see.

But you can only see a small part of the world around you (the light spectrum that is visible to us is less than a ten-trillionth of it according to David Eagleman). At a nice, simple level, there must be zillions of TV and radio waves zipping around you. Oh, and your wifi connection. But we, as humans, can't see those wavelengths. Bees probably can, which is why they're nearly extinct. And rattlesnakes see infrared.

Superman had a wider spectrum, at least in the Christopher Reeve years. Remember the early *Superman* movies where he had X-ray vision, which he only ever used once for the right reasons. He pretty much wasted it by seeing through buildings and stuff like that.

I think it's time we introduce a German scientist by the name of Jakob von Uexküll. With a name like that, you know he's a lot cleverer than Andy or me. Von Uexküll suggested the part of the world we can see and be aware of is called the *umwelt*. Essentially, that's your world. The one you can see, hear, touch, taste and smell.

And he calls the rest of it, the bigger reality, the *umgebung*. Roll that one around in your head a couple of times. '*Um-ge-bung*'. Personally, I have the need to say it aloud, just as I do the North Devon town of Georgeham. For some reason, every time I drive through Georgeham, I have so say it in a broad west country accent – '*Jaaaarr-jum*.'

We promised no big words but, technically, 'umgebung' isn't 'big'. It's only got eight letters. And 'umwelt' only six. Anyway, each species has its own umwelt, its own little world that it knows. But outside of that lives an entire earthly universe that it never considers. For example, my dog exists in a world of black and white (yes, she's a black and white dog, but what I mean is that she has no 'cones' in her eyes, so she can only see in black and white. That might explain her disinterest in snooker.) She exists in a world of smells and her hearing is a lot better than mine. She doesn't know about the FTSE100 and she's no idea that France exists. She accepts her umwelt and stops there. She accepts the reality as it is presented to her. It's her reality. She doesn't know any different.

And neither do you. Your reality is far more subjective than you suppose. Your umwelt is (hopefully) bigger than my mutt's. You, at least, will know that France exists (if not, Google it). And, here's the biggie, instead of reality being passively recorded by the brain, it is *actively constructed*.

That sentence will differ in meaning, according to how far along the spectrum of 'self-development junkie' you are. Excuse the rather obtuse 'druggie' analogy, but this book could be your first foray into 'self-help' and is therefore the equivalent of your first spliff. Or you could be a regular snorter of self-help. It helps you stay high. Or, like Andy and I, you could be completely hooked and dependent, needing your self-help fix every day. If you're a regular user, the sentence, '*instead of reality being passively recorded by the brain, it is actively constructed*' will probably be nothing new. If this is your first self-help spliff, you'll be like '*hey man, this personal development is really heavy shit.*'

Evolutionary psychology explores where our thinking came from and particularly how our thinking has enabled us to solve social problems. It's akin to modern-day apps that you download to your phone. Throughout the centuries, human brains developed and downloaded a series of apps which enabled them to solve the problems of the day. And new apps were added as we evolved. There was the 'Making Fire 1' app (MF1), which involved creating sparks by bashing flint. Then MF2, rubbing two sticks together. And MF3, Swan Vestas. And so on. But, because we're lazy creatures, we don't delete the previous app. We keep it and it adds to the rich tapestry of our brain construction. Which is why boy scouts still have the ability to rub two sticks together and create fire.[19]

Our new science of 'Quantum Psychology' is a nice, simple way of finding out who you *really* are. And it necessitates a realisation that your thoughts aren't *real*, at least not in the sense that you can put them in a wheelbarrow. For example, on similar lines to Schrödinger's Cat, you can be on holiday sunning yourself by the pool, sipping a beer, having the time of your life when your best mate texts you the football scores from home. Your team has been mullered. And that's it, you immediately feel bad.

---

[19] *I like Terry Deary's alternative, which is to rub two boy scouts together to create fire.*

But, hang on, the result happened *yesterday*. The event is over. But now, when you think about the event, you feel bad. Clearly the event itself didn't make you feel bad. Your *thoughts* about the event are the guilty party. The event was most definitely 'real' but it didn't affect how you felt until you thought about it.

Let's take another example. Imagine your 6-year-old niece was having nightmares. The poor child was weepy at bedtime because she was scared of a bogeyman in the cupboard. You wouldn't ask her to describe the bogeyman in detail and discuss what aspect she found most terrifying. And, at bedtime, you wouldn't hide in the wardrobe and leap out at her[20] or ask your niece to think about it constantly. You'd take her mind off it by focusing on something good. You'd tell your niece it was just her imagination, her *thinking*.

"Monsters under your bed? Don't worry. It's the burglars coming through your window that you need to look out for."

---

[20] *However tempting that might be.*

'Remember, some small children are frightened by fireworks. Another great way to frighten them is to tell gory ghost stories.'

Philip Ardagh

We are living in the middle of a revolution in consciousness. Over the last decade scientists have made great strides in understanding the building blocks of human flourishing. And one of the primary findings is that we are the products of what happens below the level of awareness.

Tim Wilson (University of Virginia) suggests the human mind can take in 11 million pieces of information at any given moment. So there are 11 million pieces of data vying for your conscious attention. *Pick me. Pick me.* If you were consciously aware of all of them you'd be a slobbering, gibbering wreck. The most generous estimate is that people can be consciously aware of 40 of the 11 million. I've just stabbed a few numbers on my calculator and it's struggling to work out the percentage. If Wilson's estimation is right, I reckon we're aware of 0.00036 of a percent of what's actually going on around us. By any stretch of anyone's imagination, that's a tiny fraction.

So what?

I've heard it described in various ways. The one that resonates with me is that the *conscious* mind is like a general atop a platform who sees the world from a distance and analyses things linearly and linguistically. The *unconscious* mind is like 11 million little scouts on a reconnaissance mission. The scouts scatter across the landscape, sending back a constant flow of signals. They are immersed in the environment. They scurry about, interpreting whatever they happen to come across. These scouts coat their findings with emotional significance. And, more often than not, it is the ones with the *most emotional significance* that make it into the 40 pieces of consciousness we call our 'reality'.

Jonathan Haidt suggests that these signals don't control our lives, but they shape our interpretation of the world and they guide us – rather like a spiritual sat nav.

To build on what we started in an earlier chapter, we are pre-programmed to take notice of the scouts who find danger. They send back a big, fat, emotionally-charged signal that is immediately brought to your attention. The survival principle means that danger, anger, jealousy and rage all trump happiness and joy. Which can be rather a bummer.

So it is often these negatives that jostle to the front of the queue and make it into your top 40. And, to feel better, we need to find ways of reassigning importance to the scouts who find happiness and joy, a retraining of your mental habits that we describe as simple, but not easy.

And that, dear reader, is where we're heading off to after we've revisited the glorious summer of 1976.

POOH STICKS

'I did not have three thousand pairs of shoes, I had one thousand and sixty.'

Imelda Marcos

Cast your mind back to the summer of 1976. If you're not old enough, let me paint you a picture. The summer holidays were drenched in glorious sunshine. Tarmac melted, hosepipes were banned, The Goodies ruled TV and Abba dominated the airwaves. I was 9 years old and it was the most wonderful summer ever. If you watch *Stand by Me* you'll have more of an idea. There were no social media, so me and my real flesh-and-blood friends played outside for six whole weeks. These were halcyon days of no sun-cream, paedophiles, mobile phones or cycle helmets.

We spent a lot of time playing down by the river. The drought had lowered the Trent to a trickle, so we swam, built dens and played Pooh sticks. For the uninitiated, let me explain what Pooh sticks is (thankfully, it's not as bad as it sounds). Everyone chooses a stick and lines up on a bridge, where, after a count of 3, you all drop your stick into the river and they race to the finish line. For us, that was a tree, about 50 metres downstream.

So there are half a dozen of us, lined up on the disused railway bridge, the Trent flowing below. *One . . . two . . . three . . .* the sticks fall, splashing into the river and we're off, sprinting 50 metres to the finish line to cheer our sticks on. I admit there's an element of 'you had to be there' to get the sheer magic of the moment, but please live it with me, as if you, too, were a 9-year-old in the summer of '76.

Six young lads are bellowing at their sticks as they approach the finishing tree. Eventually, my mate Pat punches the air as his stick flows over the line. '*Get in!*'

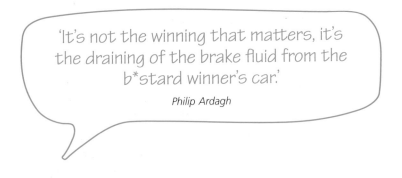

'It's not the winning that matters, it's the draining of the brake fluid from the b*stard winner's car.'

Philip Ardagh

Mick's stick comes in second and Woody's third. There's a slight delay as Warren's and then Ju's sticks float by. *And there's no sign of my stick.*

My pals start jabbering excitedly about the next race, deciding where to stand on the bridge to hit the fastest currents.

My eyes are on the river. *My stick has still not arrived*.

The lads get bored waiting for my stick and they turn and wander back to the bridge for race number 2.

And still my stick hasn't arrived.

I watch them climb back up onto the railway bridge, line up and let their sticks fall to the water for a second time.

And my first stick still hasn't arrived.

I'm 9 and I'm curious. So I march back to the bridge, but instead of climbing up it, I scramble down to the river bank, directly underneath the huge metal structure. It's colder under here and a little bit echoey. The flowing water is magnified ever so slightly. And I can see my stick, sticking out of the water. It hit the river and got stuck behind one of the legs of the bridge. My stick was doomed right from the start.

And little did I know that nearly 40 years later, my stick would make it into this book.[21] Because my Pooh stick represents how life can sometimes be. We can all get a bit stuck. Everyone else seems to be fine, but for one reason or another we're feeling as though we're struggling to move forward. Now, my take on that stick is pretty much the same as my take on society. I don't think the stick needs medication. And I doubt it needs to lie on a couch and explain why it's stuck. I think the stick just needs a little nudge. Probably only the gentlest little encouragement and it'll be away, into the flow of the river, coasting along quite nicely.

And that analogy might annoy you if you're on medication or having counselling. So be it. I'm not denigrating Prozac or Cognitive Behavioural Therapy. I know both save lives. I'm hoping that you can see my wider point – that sometimes we all require a gentle nudge to get us moving in the right direction.

---

[21] *Well, to be fair, I didn't know there would be a book.*

> 'Therapy is expensive. Bubble wrap is cheap. You choose.'
>
> *Unknown*

The analogy is enhanced by the fact that, in positive psychology, there is something called 'flow'. A state of flow is when life feels good. Things seem timeless and you are challenged in just the way you like to be challenged. You are playing to your strengths and you feel invigorated rather than exhausted. It seems to me that 'flow' is a pretty cool place to be.

Allow me to go a little deeper and relate 'flow' to some of the themes we introduced earlier. Remember, Andy and I aren't coming at this book from a religious perspective, but sometimes various Gods just kind of pop up.

Buddhism speaks of the four 'noble truths'. One of them is that 'attachment' is the root cause of all suffering. In essence, we grasp tight hold of things that we value (possessions, loved ones, employment, etc.) and try and hold on to them forever. And we push away what we don't like (in my case olives, mood hoovers, reality TV), trying to avoid them at all costs. Both constitute 'attachment'. And pain is inevitable. At some point you'll lose what you want (a loved one will pass away or, on a lesser scale, your favourite shoes will wear out). Plus, at some point I'll have to eat an olive and watch an episode of *Don't Tell the Bride*.

The next couple of sentences may seem a little philosophical, but it helps if you're able to see everything as fleeting. The world is impermanent. Your youthful good looks, for example. You need to enjoy them while you have them and not become too attached. Otherwise, you'll suffer when they fade.

Apparently (and I say 'apparently' because I'm a real-world person and am therefore struggling with this concept in its purest form), to live a non-attached life isn't about losing your feelings and impulses. It's about tuning into the feelings and impulses without becoming hooked on thoughts about how the world 'should be'. The world is as it is. Relax. It's about enjoying what you've got, while you've got it; the idea being that it leaves you calm, serene and in the moment.

'Gandhi used to walk everywhere barefoot, so his feet became painfully rough. He also had a very simple diet, which left him thin and frail, and with bad breath. All of which made him a super-calloused fragile mystic, vexed by halitosis.'

Unknown

Of course, living in the moment is easier said than done!

In our previous book, we introduced the concept of the 'happiness rainbow' and while our publishers are keen for us to move on, we think this is a concept worthy of revisiting. It won't have escaped your notice that there's been a glitch in the banking system. Not only have they lent money that they didn't have, but, to add insult to injury, they've sold us products we didn't need. Cue a massive banking crisis and yet another attempt by Germany to take over Europe.

'A German, a Greek, a Portuguese and an Irishman go into a bar.
The German pays.'

Unknown

But, to be frank, the banking crisis is just background noise. The fact that we've been mis-sold various banking products to the tune of a few billion pounds is an irrelevance compared to the ubiquitous mis-selling of happiness.

'Happiness' has been sold to you as a fantastic pot of emotional gold, buried at the end of the rainbow. It's a wonderful feeling that you want more of and it's '*over there*'. Happiness has been mis-sold as the reward, the elusive end point that we all crave. It's something you must earn, or pursue.

'I've always taken *The Wizard of Oz* very seriously, you know. I believe in the idea of the rainbow. And I've spent my entire life trying to get over it.'

Judy Garland

And the mis-selling scandal begins when you're very young. Your parents and teachers tell you that if you work hard at primary school you'll get great SATs results. And when you get those great results, guess what? *Then you'll be happy*.

And if you work hard at big school you'll get some As and A*s and *then you'll be happy*.

And you'll get a job and you'll have a sales target. And when you hit your sales target, *then you'll be happy*.

Or you'll be happy when you change jobs or, classically, you'll be happy when you're walking down the aisle with your perfect partner.

You are sold the vision of '*I'll be happy when . . .*'

In terms of tweaking your thinking, what if that's a big, fat lie? You need to claim compensation from whomever sold you this vision of happiness. What if 'happiness' is a fantastic feeling – a pot of emotional gold at the end of the rainbow – but what if it's at our end?

What if being happy *NOW* is the key to success? For example, what if it's the happiest kids that get the best results? What if it's the happiest, most upbeat salesperson that naturally gets on with people and generates the most sales, month after month? What if being happy now is the key to finding your perfect partner, because, let's face it, you're much more attractive when you're smiling?

> 'A positive attitude may not solve all your problems, but it will annoy enough people to make it worth the effort.'
>
> *Herm Albright*

And this line of inquiry leads me to a very big question, one that's already been hinted at in earlier chapters – what if we've been looking for happiness in the wrong place?

A lot of the religious, philosophical and academic literature points to *NOW* as being the best (and only) place to be happy.

Holy cow! *Now?* Wow! But *how?*

THE VENDETTA

'I play all my Country and Western music backwards – your lover returns, your dog comes back and you cease to be an alcoholic.'

Linda Smith

Wolfie, will you please do some violin practice

After I've finished this level

It was doing Mr Mozart's head in

I'd like to delve a bit deeper into the spam filter analogy from earlier. This might take a bit of wrestling with, but what you pay attention to becomes your life.

Maureen Gaffney suggests that attention is the crucial gateway between us and the world around us, between the events that happen *to* us and what happens *within* us. Essentially, it's not the stream of daily events that registers in your consciousness, it is only what you pay attention to. To boil this down to the basics, *you* create your world.

I adore Robert Holden's concept of the 'beautiful ordinary'. I'll wager that the top 10 happiest moments of your life are *experiences* rather than products. And Robert's point is that happiness is available to you every second of the day and it resides in things that are simple and free. But you have to open yourself up to the possibility of looking at the right end of the rainbow. Happiness is already here! *Hooray!*

But, hang on, I'm looking out of the window at the greyness of the autumnal day and I'm wondering, are you sure Robert? Are you sure I don't have to wait until the weather cheers up a bit?

The 'beautiful ordinary' concept has never been more certain, because the top 10 happiest moments of your entire life will be a whole list of weirdly simple pleasures and experiences. Like looking out of the window and *noticing* that the autumn leaves are turning yellow, red and gold. *Simple and free.*

Or playing Pooh sticks in the summer of '76. *Simple and free.*

Or being on the giving or receiving end of a twizzle (when someone grabs your arms and spins you round).[22] *Simple and free.*

[22] My dad used to do twizzles the other way around. He'd grab my feet and twizzle me, so all the blood rushed to my head and my eyes bulged out of their sockets. Highly recommended.

Or camping in the rain when you were 8 years old. *Simple and almost free.*

Or winning the egg and spoon race at school. *Simple and free.*

Or your child taking her first steps. *Simple and free.*

Or watching a spectacular thunderstorm. *Simple and free.*

(Tell me when I'm boring you.)

Hugging your teenage daughter when she comes back from university. *Simple and free.*

Building a camp fire. *Simple and free.*

Your first proper kiss. *Simple and free* (the 'price' might depend on who you kiss, to be fair).

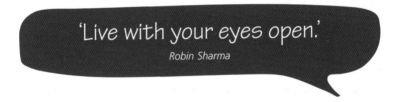

'Live with your eyes open.'
Robin Sharma

I've tried to add a modicum of humour to Robert's 'beautiful ordinary'. But it's not funny. If you 'get it', it's profound. I spent many years getting it wrong. When my kids were little I'd take them to the park and they'd be let loose on the swings and slides. They'd be having a joyous time until I decided *I'd* had enough. 'Come on you two, time to go.'

Of course, they didn't want to go home. They were having the time of their lives. 'Why have we got to go, daddy?'

'I'm not sure. We just have,' I'd say, dragging them away.

The 'beautiful ordinary' philosophy means I should have enjoyed the moment. I should have sat and luxuriated in watching my kids having fun, for as long as it took. Even better, I should have joined in, enthusiastically. Sure, I'd have been the only grown-up on the monkey bars, my adult backside would have slowed my downward trajectory on the slide and I'd have felt a bit sick on the swings – but hey, myself and the kids would have been living in the joyous moment of now. It could well have made it into the top 10 happiest moments of my life. And theirs!

> 'Give the mundane its beautiful due.'
> John Updike

I describe being happy in the moment as 'simple but not easy'. Let me introduce you to something you've experienced but have never known what to call. Something that knocks us off being our best self.

I asked an audience to come up with an example of a little thing that irritates them a lot.

'My wife,' offered a gentleman on the back row.

'What aspect particularly annoys you?' I asked, wishing I hadn't.

'When she breathes,' he snarled.

Look here folks, I'm not the Dalai Lama. And while Andy W might have put on a couple of pounds, he ain't Buddha. We're normal guys living in the same crazy world as everyone else. We're not saintly. We do get it wrong. We do get irritated. Living a happy life that 'goes with the flow' can be tricky. The pot of happiness gold in the NOW can be elusive.

Let me give you an example that might make you want to throw this book away in disgust.

It's Tuesday and I've dedicated the entire day to working on my thesis. I've taken the trouble to drive to Loughborough and have secreted myself in the library. This is a vast building. The entrance and first floor are dedicated noisy areas full of student chatter and clinking of Costa coffee cups. Downstairs is the quiet area, more of a traditional library, where we work like Trappist monks, silence being the order of the day. And it's here that I'm situated, books spread, laptop booted, bottled water at the ready, my learning head on. Happiness is right here, right now.

A guy wearing headphones wanders past. *Headphones in a library?* I find this mildly irritating but everybody else is wearing them too, so I'm clearly in the wrong millennium. *Get over it Andy.*

Mr Headphones sits in the cubicle next to me. *That's fine.* He wrestles with his rucksack and is soon arranged a bit like me, laptop and books at the ready. *He's choosing to study with his headphones on. That's fine too.* I get on with my calculations but my happiness rating has been downgraded from 'effusive' to 'hanging in there'.

The guy then wrestles with a packet of crisps and starts crunching them. I look at the sign that says '*no eating or* drinking, except bottled water'. It's as crystal clear as my bottled water. There's something about headphone wearing that makes you unaware of how loud you're being. I knew from experience that once, when I was wearing headphones, I accidentally shouted. What I was about to learn is that when you eat crisps the crunching echoes in your mouth up through your nasal cavity and is magnified in your head.

Mr Headphones is unaware of this fact as he slips into a consistent pattern. There's severe rustling as his hand goes into the crisp packet, followed by magnified munching as crisps are masticated. And, believe you me, he's masticating like mad.

I'm in the middle of writing my thesis. It's important. *Carry on working, carry on working. He's eating crisps. It's not a big deal.* My happiness rating? 'At risk'.

Rustle, crunch, crunch; rustle, crunch, crunch . . .

AAAAgghhhhh!

But it's okay because there's a librarian coming our way. Everyone knows that you can have food and drink *upstairs* but not down here. I glance at the sign for reassurance. I don't need to report him. '*Please miss, he's eating crisps,*' would be churlish. I'm confident that the librarian knows the rules so will ask him to stop. I hold my breath as she comes closer. His crunching stops and she walks right past.

And he starts again!

My happiness has morphed into rage.

In the big scheme of my life, was it a big deal? No.

Did I want to bash him to a pulp with a really heavy thesis? Yes!

Now, you could read the last paragraph of that anecdote and dismiss this entire book.

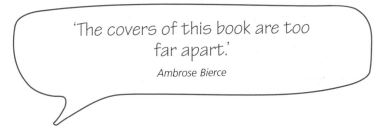

> 'The covers of this book are too far apart.'
> Ambrose Bierce

You could argue, quite easily, that whatever we're peddling doesn't work. The author wants to beat an innocent student to death because he's eating his lunch noisily. That's most definitely *not* positive thinking.[23]

Or you could say, do you know what, that's real life. It's an example of tiny, trivial stuff that chips away at us and knocks us off being brilliant. Andy and I think it's OK to have a few bad moments. It's all part of being human. So long as that's all they are. *Moments*.

If 'anger', 'irritability', 'rage' and 'grumpiness' are your default emotions, then there's a bit more work to do. If you regularly give the one-finger salute to your fellow motorists, then you'll find value in what we're saying. If beating people senseless with big textbooks is your thing, then you're going to need more than this book (it's not really big enough to hit people with, for a start).

The library episode is an example of what's called *Vipassana Vendetta*. If you're going to drop that into conversation you'd

---

[23] *Those who are really switched on will also be thinking that it'd make an awful lot of noise so, if you were going to beat him senseless, you'd be better off doing it on the upper floor where the noise levels are more relaxed.*

better know what it means. Vipassana Vendetta is the magnification of tiny irritations into full-blown hate campaigns. And it goes some way to explaining why it's often the tiniest things that annoy us the most.

So getting narked by having to show my boarding pass when buying a Toblerone is perfectly normal. As is getting irritated by over-cautious health and safety notices in public washrooms. 'Caution, hot water' at the hot tap, for example. *You don't effing say!*

Or an A4 poster showing me how to wash my hands. *Do I really need pictures?*

So, if the world is chucking a whole load of negatives at us, the question is how do I stop myself getting ground down? What can I do to rescue myself from *myself*? Most of us have got plenty of big things to be grappling with, never mind Vipassana and his personal vendetta of minutiae, designed to tip us over the edge.

Well, Andy and I rather like the simplicity of reframing. I appreciate that this may not be new information, but it's simple and effective and therefore warrants a reminder. A reframe is when you look at the world from a different perspective and often requires you to ask a better question. It can be a teensy bit Pollyannaish, so be careful not to overdo it.

'Wowza, grandma's died. What an excellent opportunity to go to a funeral. Think of those yummy sandwiches!' is almost certainly a reframe too far.

But, *'Grandma's died. How gut-wrenchingly sad. But I'm so glad I knew her for so long and loved and appreciated her while I could,'* is probably about right.

'Nan would always send us texts saying please come round, my angina is getting worse; but then they stopped. So presumably it got better.'

Gary Delaney

So, in a nutshell, reframes move you from 'dwelling on the negative' to 'appreciating the positive'. They get easier with practice. Here are a few for you to consider:

Situation	Reframe
Your teenager is glued to his X-Box	At least he's at home and not wandering the streets
You seem to be paying a lot of tax	I earn money
Your lawn needs mowing and the gutter needs fixing	I have a house
The supermarket car park is just about full, so you have to park at the far end	I can walk
You have a pile of washing and ironing to do	I have clothes
(One for kids) You have mountains of homework	I'm getting an education
The alarm goes off at 6am	I'm alive!

YOUR HAPPINESS ALLOWANCE

'The tragedy of modern discontent is that it is largely created by ourselves – by our culture and its mindset. Originating in a system of mass production which generates vast quantities of products which need to be sold, it is the marketeers' ambition to make us feel dissatisfied with what we already possess, to make us feel that we'd be happier, or more attractive, if we went out to purchase one or more of their products . . . That culture insidiously feeds our discontent, our restlessness, our dissatisfaction. However many products we choose to buy, more never proves enough. However much we accumulate, there is always another, higher level of dissatisfaction.'

John Lane, Timeless Simplicity, Green Books, 2002, p.99

When you book with an airline they give you a baggage allowance, the maximum you can take on board. And happiness and positivity can work in a similar way. Before we look more closely at strategies you can use for feeling brilliant, it's worth examining just how happy you're *allowed* to be. Or *supposed* to be.

Wandering around Cheshire Cat style, grinning inanely for no apparent reason is not socially acceptable.[24] If you're overly

---

[24] I tried it in the public toilets at Markeaton Park and narrowly avoided a George Michael type situation.

happy, you will annoy people or they will think you're fake or, even worse, they will deem you simple.

Your psychology and physiology has a mechanism to guard against *extreme* happiness. And, as always, I want to give a different slant on things, so I thought I'd link it to having a hot bath.

I have a theory. Women have hotter baths than men. They seem to be able to withstand scalding temperatures. So hot, in fact, that they go pink!

Conversely, men cope better in the cold British sea. Women, as a rule, don't get further than their knees. Men, on the other hand, brave it until they are bluey-purple.

So what? In hot baths and cold seas, there is an initial shock to the system. It's painful, at least for a minute or two. The British sea can be so achingly cold that you strut round, chicken-style, with oval mouth and wide eyes. Your body soon adapts. It becomes accustomed to the extreme temperature and your physiology compensates. In the cold sea, your body's reflex mechanism is to keep you warm, so most of your blood goes to your core, leaving you blue on the outside. Conversely, the hot bath reflex is for your body to try and lose heat, so it moves all your blood vessels to the surface and you develop a pinky glow. You don't have to think about this. It just happens.[25]

And 'happiness' works on more or less the same basis. We all have what scientists call a 'set point'. This is your *default* happiness setting. Things can happen which cause you to rise

---

[25] *Obviously, this only applies to white people. I'm not entirely sure what colour black people go. Maybe someone can email me or send me a pic of a black guy in the sea at Mablethorpe?*

above your set point. Think lottery win, wedding, birth of a grandchild or passing an exam. Equally, awful things can happen that cause you to fall below your default happiness setting. The death of a loved one, a relationship break-up, redundancy or illness, for example.

But, just as in a hot bath, your body compensates and your happiness levels out. So, according to science, we are able to experience small bursts of extreme happiness but striving to be happier forever is a waste of time. The set point acts like a string of elastic, pulling you back to where it thinks you *should* be. The set point is useful because it stops us living in happiness utopia and it also helps us bounce back after a bout of awfulness.

So, according to the boffins, you cannot therefore affect long-term happiness because you'll always be dragged back to your set point.

But what if we're missing a trick and your happiness 'set point' isn't, in fact, 'set'? What if we could find ways of raising the bar so that your 'normal' happiness was set a little higher? What if your happiness thermostat was turned up, just a notch or two, into the 'feeling like I can take on the world' zone?

Various scientific studies concur that most people are in the Goldilocks zone of *mildly happy most of the time*. There's even a phrase, 'happy medium' (no, not a giggling fortune teller), which describes a happiness compromise. Not too happy and not too sad.

I genuinely think there's room for improvement, and while '*deliriously joyful, always and forever*' would be absurd, '*very happy most of the time*' would be worth a punt.

So, if you'll allow me to follow the fishing line to the bottom of the academic ocean, I find the 'hedonic treadmill' and its close cousin, 'habituation'. These are examples of academic oysters I mentioned earlier, real bastards to get into but really rewarding when you've made the effort.

'If money can fix it, it's not a problem.'

Rita Davenport

Let's start with the hedonic treadmill. It's actually a pretty cool term. You're familiar with running on a treadmill. You run and run and run and run and then you get off. And where have you gone? *Absolutely bloody nowhere*. Similarly, we are chasing the highs of happiness but, according to the hedonic treadmill, are doomed to come back to square one, our predetermined set point. Receiving what you wanted doesn't really make you happy. You wanted a good education, you got one, you're not happy. You wanted a partner, got one, still not happy. Thousands of times you got exactly what you wanted, and you're still only *mildly happy most of the time!*

You can buy a watch for £10 or £10,000. They both tell the time, albeit the expensive one will tell you the time at 300 fathoms. Why would you buy a watch for £10,000? Apart from the obvious answer 'because you've got 10 grand to spare', the other answer is that it makes you feel good. You're deriving feelings from 'stuff'. I don't doubt there's a short-term frisson of excitement when you buy 'stuff'. The problem is that the hedonic treadmill means you have to keep buying things to maintain your happiness. This is the treadmill aspect of the term. You're not really getting anywhere, other than in debt!

'I have a chef, 24-hour security, five cars . . . apart from that I don't need anything.'

Robbie Williams

Research shows that buying *stuff* doesn't equate to long-term happiness.[26] If you want to squeeze more from your happiness pound, you're better off buying an *experience*. A trip to the theatre, for example. Or a concert, a holiday or a meal out – the theory says that they will score you plenty of happiness brownie points. Furthermore, the best way to maximise your happiness is to indulge in a series of smaller purchases rather than one whopper. So, for example, you'll score more on the 'happy-ometer' from going to loads of local gigs rather than one splurge at the O₂. Or, similarly, several smaller holidays to Llandudno rather than one trip to the Maldives (that's probably where the whole theory collapses!).

Three points that warrant further consideration:

1. Stay within your budget. Over-spending creates stress and lowers your happiness.

---

[26] *Yes, yes, if you're a real boffin you'll know that there's a link between 'income' and 'life satisfaction' and 'life satisfaction' includes elements of happiness, so I'm splitting hairs.*

2. Don't blow all your money on one event. You are better having loads of curry nights rather than one big blowout at the Ritz.

3. Buying new golf clubs won't bring you happiness. But hitting a superb tee-shot with them will.

'Habituation' is subtly different. This is where something starts off as exciting but the effect gradually wears off. This is why young children live in a permanent state of 'wowza!' Everything's novel.

'Puddle!' *Splash*. 'Cooool.'

'Cardboard box.' *Climb in*. 'Wicked, it's a rocket!'

That's why young children run everywhere. They're excited about life because everything's new and exciting.

> 'We don't stop playing because we get old, we get old because we stop playing.'
>
> George Bernard Shaw

And, as we mature, we develop a habit of been-there-done-that. Nothing's new any more.

Puddle? 'Err, no. Don't splash in that, it's cold and wet and silly.'

As for making a rocket ship out of a cardboard box. Well, that's just childish.

Exactly!

> 'The world is mud-luscious and puddle-wonderful.'
>
> *E. E. Cummings*

It's going to sound rather odd, but one of the secrets to feeling great is to get excited about things. Not ridiculously. We don't want you wetting your pants. Just dare to ratchet up your levels of enthusiasm a couple of notches.

Here's an example of habituation. I am lucky enough to have a successful series of children's books in shops.[27] I remember the day when the first book came out. We were on holiday in Devon and we rushed to the local book shop, banging on the door at 9am. We rushed in, found the children's section and my daughter swept all the Harry Potter books off a shelf and arranged the *Spy Dog* books face on. We grinned all day.

Book 2 was exciting too.

Book 3 was all right . . .

Last week was the launch of book 15. *My kids don't even know it exists.*

That's habituation in action. It's also one of the reasons why a pay rise doesn't lead to long-term motivation. It's exciting on pay slip number 1, but then we just get used to it. It's why people

---

[27] *What do you mean, I've already mentioned that? I'll jolly well be mentioning it again soon!*

who live by the sea aren't excited by the sea but us land-lubbers cheer when we see it. It's why Londoners get ground down because they do the hustle and bustle every day. Us northerners love a trip to the smoke!

It's why we need to put a bit of effort into being more positive and enthusiastic. I ran a session for some professional footballers and they moaned about their jobs. 'Training, training, match. Training, training, match . . .'

Love can be the same. Habituation means the passion can simply wear off.

Here's an interesting test. If you want to find out who loves you more, your partner or your dog, lock them both in the boot of your car for two hours and when you open the boot, see who is more pleased to see you!

Even your life itself can become habituated, see my reference to Dull in Scotland in an earlier chapter. Life can become a bit like that.

Habituation also has a more sinister side. Philip Zimbardo links it to 'arousal addiction', particularly in boys. Most drug addicts start off on party pills or smoking a bit of weed. It's deemed to be exciting but nothing more than a bit of harmless fun. Habituation means you soon become accustomed to the high and seek something a bit higher.

Yum yum, a line of coke, and wham, before you know it, you're a crack addict in a bedsit cooking spaghetti hoops on a camping stove.

I don't want to get too heavy, but the same process of habituation applies to internet pornography. Teenage boys go through a phase when their brains are focused on novelty, excitement and constant arousal. They will seek arousal via the readily available sexual imagery of the internet. 'Normal' sex becomes habituated. They seek higher highs and normal, loving sex becomes dull.

Our plea is to be careful lads and lasses. In a world of easy access to just about anything, the 'anything' might ruin your long-term relationships.

MULLETS AND BANANAS

The Glow-worm Song
'I wish I was a glow worm,
a glow worm's never glum,
cos how can you be grumpy,
when the sun shines out your bum?'

Anonymous

We have tried to avoid traditional 'positive thinking' stuff, or at least tried to put a realistic spin on it throughout this book, and hopefully the message is starting to sink in that true, long-lasting happiness, positivity and effervescence come from within.

If you change your internal world, your external world changes, or at least your *experience* of the external world will change. Focus on the good things in your life and you roll the dice in your favour. You've improved your odds of feeling good. And vice versa. But, to summarise the essence of our evolutionary struggle, bad weighs more than good (remember, fear saves your life whereas happiness merely enriches it), so we are therefore naturally drawn to notice negativity.

There is one 'thing' that will have a really big impact on your world. A 'thing' that gets a mention in every half-decent self-help book ever written. A 'thing' that isn't actually a 'thing' at all – that 'thing' being your beliefs.

Beliefs are a big deal. A belief is something in your head that you hold to be true. You have a model of the world that you hold in your head. You 'know' what's right and what's wrong, what's acceptable and what's unacceptable. You might have religious beliefs. Or you might think religion is a load of old nonsense. Both of you are right. You might have a belief that you should get up and go to work and earn an honest living and that people on benefits are scroungers. Or you might be on benefits and have a belief that life's a bitch and there are no jobs. Or you might be on benefits and be wondering why on Earth people get up at 6am and commute to work when they could be sitting at home watching daytime telly. You're right again!

When I was 13 I remember my gran telling me that the people on telly could see you watching them! Holy smoke. I was so embarrassed, I never watched *Baywatch* again!

If you change a belief, you will change your experience of the world. The tricky bit is, for most people, we *believe* our beliefs are real, which makes them really hard to change.

Good news! Beliefs are not real, we have learned them. Essentially, your beliefs are based on your past experience.

In our own inimitable style, here's an example from the Oceanic Institute in Woodhouse, Atlanta. We've broken it down into manageable steps in case you want to replicate this experiment at home with your kids.

- Get yourself a 20,000 gallon fish tank.
- While in the pet shop, you will also need a barracuda (nasty-looking fish that killed Nemo's mum).[28] Oh, and a mullet (that's a type of fish, not a hair-do).
- If you're doing this with your kids, I always feel it's nice to give the fish names so they have some emotional attachment to the experiment, so we'll go for 'Barry the Barracuda' and 'Molly the Mullet'.
- Next, fill the tank with water and throw Barry and Molly in. Observe Molly's body language. She will eye-ball Barry and her fins will wilt because she knows, and Barry knows, that barracudas eat mullet. It's their absolute favourite food. Typically, your kids might squeal and hide their faces at this stage.
- Tell your kids, quite sternly, that life's not fair and, in fact, nobody ever said it was. This is something they will have to get to grips with when they get to big school, so you may as well expose them to reality early doors.
- Before Barry can have his mullet breakfast, take a glass screen and slide it down the middle of the fish tank so Barry is on one side and Mol on the other.
- Now, Barry can see Molly and Molly can see Barry. Barry is thinking 'Eh up' (he's a northern barracuda) 'there's a tasty bit of mullet over there,' and, with a flip of his tail, he shoots across the tank and smashes his fishy face on the glass screen.
- 'Ecky thump! (we've pinpointed 'northern' to a more exact location . . . Barnsley). Barry has a headache and there's barracuda snot on the screen.
- Barry is a really hungry killer-fish, so he isn't going to let one failure hold him back. He circles his side of the tank

---

[28] Apologies if that's a plot spoiler. But at least he gets reunited with his dad at the end. Phew!

163

and flips his tail again. Molly holds her breath,[29] awaiting her fate. Barry smashes against the glass a second time.

- *'Blood and effing sand. This mullet eating isn't what it used to be.'* Your kids will be cheering because, against all odds, Molly has survived. Tell them to shut up. Build the suspense. Tell them it ain't over yet. Barry's good looks might have gone but he's a determined little so-and-so.

- There are rumbles in his barracuda tumbles, so Barry circles for a final attempt and really goes for it. Your kids will be watching from behind their hands as he propels across the tank like a torpedo. If he had been going any faster when he hit the screen the only thing that would have gone through his mind would have been his arse. *Smash!* Dazed, confused and bloodied, Barry swims back round now thinking, *'Eating mullet hurts your face.'*

- Now here comes the interesting bit. After the third attempt you can remove the screen and, although Barry can now easily swim across, he doesn't. In fact (and your kids will be amazed at this), Barry would rather starve than go into Molly's side of the tank! In a 'fun-for-all-the-family' experiment, your kids can watch Barry wither and die.

- After you've flushed Barry's emaciated body down the loo, chat the experiment through with your 7-year-old. *The screen has gone, so why on Earth would Barry starve himself to death?*

Yes, dear reader, Barry's new belief system (*'eating mullet hurts your face'*) has changed his behaviour.

---

[29] *Yes, I know, technically not possible. Jog on!*

All of this begs the question, what beliefs are holding you back? What have you *accidentally* learned that's stopping you being awesome? Personal development isn't just about doing new things. It's equally about stopping doing rubbish things!

You'll have gathered that Andy and I are firmly rooted in the real world. Looking out of my window, it's not *The Little House on the Prairie*. Life can be tough, so we're not going to tell you that *anything* is possible. But, by having a positive belief system and a Bob the Builder 'can-do' attitude, a world of possibilities will open up.

'All monkeys learn to fear snakes by viewing an old monkey being scared by a snake.'

Unknown

Let's switch from barracudas to primates. The same principle as above, but it takes us slightly farther into the forest of beliefs.

How do you catch a monkey? Sounds like the start of a joke but, read on, this is true.

First, to catch a monkey, you have to go to a place where monkeys live (i.e. the jungle) and dig a hole in the ground. You then fit a cage into the hole and place a piece of fruit in the cage. Whoever sets the trap then retreats behind a tree and waits. Said primate will gambol through the forest, see the fruit and think, '*Yum yum, I like fruit*'. Our furry friend will then reach in and grab the prize. But the cage has been designed so that the primate can't get the fruit through the bars. Picture one bamboozled baboon, confused chimp or muddled macaque – its arm is in the cage, fruit grasped tightly, but it's unable to get the food into its mouth.

The monkey-catcher doesn't have to creep out, really quietly, and pounce on the animal. He or she can simply saunter up to the puzzled primate, as loud as you like, and capture it. *'Gotcha! Lifetime in zoo for you.'*

The creature can see the man approaching and knows it's going to get caught. *Yikes!* All it has to do is let go of the fruit and do a runner. But, here's the rub, the monkey would rather hang on to the fruit and get caught.

Which, once again, leads us onto a really interesting metaphorical question: how many bananas do we have in our heads? How many negative thoughts do you continue to think – thoughts that aren't serving you well but you continue to think them anyway?

- 'I'm rubbish at so-and-so.'
- 'I'm sooo stupid.'
- 'I'm too old to go for that promotion.'
- 'I'm too young to go for that promotion.'
- 'I'm not good enough to go for that promotion.'
- 'I'm not confident enough.'
- 'I'm not clever enough.'
- 'Only 25 years until retirement.'
- 'I'm stuck.'

Or behaviours? Things that you actually continue to do even though you know they're doing you no good:

- Watching too much trashy TV.
- Eating too much junk food.
- I'll have an extra 15 minutes in bed rather than doing any exercise.
- Walking with slumped shoulders instead of having a spring in your step.
- When someone asks how you are, you reply, 'Not too bad, considering.'

Just as in the monkey story, we all need to let go! Here's a startling realisation (not!). . . . the biggest thing stopping you being brilliant is YOU!

Of course, it's almost impossible to let go of a belief you don't know you have. That sentence sounds odd, but beliefs are so ingrained that, often, they've become such a part of you, so entrenched, that you're not aware that you've made them up. So, highlighting what your metaphorical bananas actually are and thinking them through is actually a great starting point.

Let me give you a real-life example. My wife's a teacher and although it's a nice enough school, it's exhausting. Since teacher training college, she's had a belief that, 'You can't teach kids on a Friday afternoon, especially not if it's windy.'

I can empathise. I know exactly what she means. And every Friday breakfast she looks out of the window and assesses the weather. 'OMG! Look at those trees, bent double. I've got no chance this afternoon. I'll just have to put Monsters Inc on again, and survive until 3.30.'

A windy Friday afternoon is a bloody great banana. She will never engage those kids in any other way while she's holding on to that belief. She needs to look out of the window on Friday morning and say *'Awesome! Look at those trees, bent double. What a fabulous opportunity for me to do something totally engaging that knocks their socks off.'*

Let go! Changing the belief changes the thinking. The new thinking invigorates the behaviour *et voila!* Everyone benefits.

Carol Dweck and Shawn Achor are both in my Panini sticker album[30] of *'heroes of personal development'*. And while some are historical heroes with black and white or sepia photos, Carol and Shawn are both full colour, current, alive and very 'now'.

I love how their thinking entwines. Carol Dweck has studied what she calls fixed and growth mind-sets. A fixed mind-set is inhibitive *'I'd better not try that in case I fail'* kind of thinking. Hence, people with fixed mind-sets tend to exist well within their comfort zones. Life can pass them by while they stay safely and securely within their potential.

A growth mind-set is more expansive. I'm summing up mightily but something like *'Life looks like a great adventure, let's give it a really good go.'* The result is that they do things and stretch themselves. They tend to squeeze much more value out of their days.

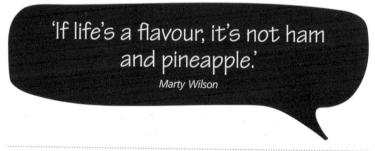

'If life's a flavour, it's not ham and pineapple.'

Marty Wilson

[30] *You have to be a 70s child, and most probably male, to understand this reference.*

168

Dweck's philosophy flowed from a study of children. She separated children into fixed and growth mind-set groups and gave both sets of kids some really tough puzzles.

Those with the fixed mind-set quickly became disheartened and began to denigrate their abilities and blame their lack of intelligence for the failures, saying things like, 'I guess I'm not very smart after all,' or 'I never did have a good memory'. What was so striking about this was that only moments before, these students had had an unbroken string of successes. Their intelligence and memory were working just fine. According to Dweck, 'they lost faith in their intellect . . . two thirds of them showed a clear deterioration in their strategies . . . the majority of students in this group abandoned or became incapable of deploying effective strategies in their repertoire.'

The growth mind-set children didn't focus on reasons for their failures. In Dweck's own surprised words, 'In fact, they didn't even consider themselves to be failing.'

When the going got tough, they kept going. They improved the quality of their strategies. A few of them even managed to solve problems that were supposedly beyond them.

The gap in performance was nothing to do with intelligence or motivation. The gap in performance was due to beliefs or mind-set. Those who believed that ability was transformable through effort not only persevered but actually improved in the teeth of difficulties. Grit and determination may not be sexy, but they shone through. Those who believed intelligence was something you either had or hadn't, floundered very quickly.

Of course, what you learn as a child becomes part of your belief system. Here's a revelation – you are, after all, just a big kid! So, is your outlook 'fixed' or 'growth'?

'I've missed more than 9000 shots. I've lost almost 300 games. 26 times I've been entrusted to take the winning game shot, and missed. That is why I succeed.'

Michael Jordan

Shawn Achor builds on this. Think of life as having two paths: one leading to mediocrity, the other to excellence. The path to mediocrity is temptingly flat and straight. Nice and easy. We can cruise along on autopilot with smooth and almost effortless progression. As Achor suggests, 'You will arrive at mediocrity with time to spare.'

The path to excellence couldn't be more different. It's like a mountain path in the Andes. The one that Jeremy Clarkson navigates in a *Top Gear* special. It's steep and gruelling with a sheer drop. It's longer too, requiring concentration and effort.

A growth mind-set is suited to this harder road. A fixed mind-set is perfect for the road to mediocrity. The spark that ignites you will be extinguished at the first sign of failure.

Here are some of Carol Dweck's mind-set characteristics:

Growth mind-set: Open to new ideas
                    Always learning (especially from setbacks)
                    Enjoy challenges
                    Believe that abilities develop

> Believe that people and lives develop
> Work at relationships

Fixed mind-set: Believe that ability and intelligence are innate
Judgemental
Limit achievement (challenge and adversity scare you)
Believe that if a relationship needs work it must be wrong
Believe that if you have to work at things you must be stupid. It should come naturally.

A group of flamingoes is called a flamboyance.

Also, a group of pugs is called a grumble.

Are they living up and down (respectively) to their collective names?

I'm going to return to this theme in the next chapter but, for now, understand the power of beliefs and the words you say to yourself. Your words create your world!

THE TRAUMA OF BEING ZAK

'Problems are lazy buggers . . . and if you go on ahead of them they often don't have enough energy to catch you up.'

Richard Wilkins

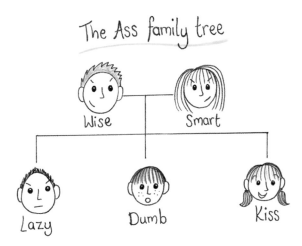

The Ass family tree

Wise   Smart

Lazy   Dumb   Kiss

You've heard of the saying, 'What doesn't kill you makes you stronger.'

That may well depend on whether you've got a fixed or growth mind-set. You will be familiar with 'post-traumatic stress disorder', a mental replay of a terrible event that happened in your past but is blighting your present. You think back to it and, *whoosh*, you're flooded with the same terrible cocktail of emotions as though it was happening again and again. PTSD seems to be very common and it courts publicity because you can claim compensation for it.

You've probably not heard of the opposite, 'post-traumatic growth', sometimes called 'adversarial growth'. That's because of our old adage that 'bad' weighs more than 'good'. Plus you can't sue somebody for improving your life.

So, for example, you often hear of soldiers who have suffered in war zones and are struggling with PTSD. You don't hear of the soldiers who return to civilian life enhanced by what they've experienced, stronger and more resilient.

It's not just about soldiers. I don't want to get too heavy, but a lump in your breast can be the end of your world or the start of it. Some people mentally bounce back and some don't.

So, the question arises, what distinguishes the people who find growth in these experiences from the people who don't? Mind-set! And something that screams out from my own research, *CHOICE!*

Positive interpretation, reframes, acceptance . . . it's all pretty much the same thing. The next sentence isn't going to seem particularly earth-shattering, but I promise you, it is.

174

Positive people use mental strategies that help them move forward.

Achor purports that this isn't just about bouncing *back* from adversity, it's about bouncing *forward*. And, once again, he's right and we bow to his genius.

Consider this scenario: you're on a plane, heading to see your sister in New Zealand. You are strapped in, taxiing for take-off and there's a faint whiff of smoke as the wheels leave the tarmac. The plane climbs, circles once and the whiff has turned into billowing black smoke. Panic ensues and the pilot makes a very heavy landing. There are 200 people on board and all of them survive. There are a few injuries and you are taken to hospital with a broken leg.

Are you lucky or unlucky?

This kind of scenario links to your 'explanatory style' and this has a crucial impact on your current and future happiness.

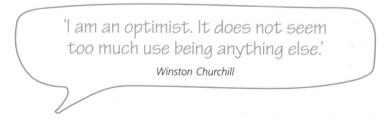

'I am an optimist. It does not seem too much use being anything else.'

Winston Churchill

An optimistic explanatory style interprets adversity as local and temporary ('It's only a broken leg, could have been an awful lot worse, and as soon as it's better I'll go and see my sis.')

A pessimistic style is described as global and permanent ('I've been seriously injured in a plane crash; it's a disaster. I will seek compensation because I can't ever fly again. My sister will have to visit me.')

As you can see, the belief generated by this event directly affects your actions. A permanently pessimistic outlook means things are bad and aren't likely to get any better, so you sink into what Martin Seligman calls 'learned helplessness'. This is when life can get very heavy indeed.

I appreciate that the emergency landing example is extreme. But you will have thousands of other incidents in your life that you are applying strategies to.

'It is not because things are difficult that we do not dare. It is because we do not dare that things are difficult.'

Seneca

In terms of 'bouncing forward' from adversity, it's a matter of retraining yourself to have a more positive explanatory style. There's a saying something akin to '*it's never too late to have a brilliant childhood*' which (I think) means that it's possible to reframe events in such a way that you learn from them rather than being traumatised by them.

I appreciate that it's not always easy. Have a quick go. Cast your mind back to a difficult time. What did you learn? How did you change? What in your life has changed for the better because of this? Is there anything about the difficult experience that you can, on reflection, be grateful for?

A researcher with a name that sounds like an address, Acacia Parks, says that the positive psychology brand of optimism is not about being positive all the time but about *'entertaining the possibility that things could work out.'* The benefit of optimism comes from being open to it, not from blindly following it even when it makes no sense to do so.

Life is a series of linear events. Then you have a chain of choices about those events, which leads to more events. And your explanatory style can trap you in a never-ending cycle of pain or free you into an upward spiral of pleasure and growth.

When the sun shines, it shines on everyone. When it rains, it rains on us all. At some point in their lives, every single person will experience tragedy, failure, rejection, depression and hopelessness.

> 'Dying is easy, it's living that scares me to death.'
>
> *Annie Lennox*

The reasons for feeling negative about yourself are numerous. Growing up in a dysfunctional family. The criticism of an insensitive teacher. Comparing yourself to, and competing with, others. Being bullied. Poor old Andy W was always the last to be picked at netball.

The reasons don't matter, they're history. What matters is now. This present moment. What do you do now to change your life?

Let me delve into deeply rooted beliefs that hold people back. I don't think there's much humour to be had here, but it's important, so please soldier on. If you have a pessimistic explanatory style and/or a fixed mind-set, there's a big fat chance that you will live *down* to your own expectations.

Example? 'The Art of Brilliance' has a burgeoning school portfolio. Delivering in businesses is great, but there's something doubly rewarding about working with kids.[31] In the UK, there seems to be a clear link between 'free school meals' and kids who underperform academically and socially. Now, I'm not going to plant the idea that maybe the free school meals are *causing* the underperformance and that there's something lurking in that punk custard that inhibits learning. That'd just be silly. *So stop thinking it!* For 'free school meals' read 'means-tested families who are probably struggling financially'.

Which leaves me scratching my head. Why does being a bit short of money mean you learn less at school? I genuinely don't get it. Unless, of course, the language you hear around you reinforces stereotypical behaviours and you live *down* to expectations. 'My mum is on benefits so I'm *supposed* to underperform at school. That's just how it is.'

Is it? Is it really?

It's certainly not how it has to be.

---

[31] *Just so you know, it can be hair-tearingly frustrating too.*

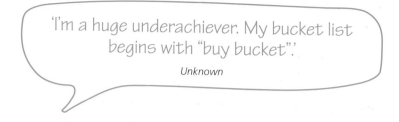

'I'm a huge underachiever. My bucket list begins with "buy bucket".'

Unknown

I'm sure the educational gurus and psychologists will be screaming at me for over-simplifying, but, get this. I delivered some 'Art of Being Brilliant' sessions in India. And the 'free school meals' kids were outperforming the others. Their explanatory style was different. *'Mum and dad are church-mice poor and I don't want to be. And the key to not being poor is to work my arse off at school and claw myself out of poverty.'* Growth mind-sets! It was bliss. The kids were a joy.

Here's a small, but potentially significant, fact-ette. Research shows that the closer your initials are to the beginning of the alphabet, the more successful you'll be. As a general rule, I promise you, this is true. As 'Andy Cope', I'm warming to this theory. Maybe there's something in it?

And, this is true, a few months back I attended a school reunion. We all had a few beers and a reminisce. You can't help but compare your lives. Towards the end of the evening, one of my old school chums had had enough of the comparisons. He sat, sobbing, 'Everyone's more successful than me. I've achieved nothing . . .'

And I said, 'Zak, I think I might know what your problem is.'

The message? You will live up (or down) to whatever stereotype you have of yourself. If your view of yourself ain't working, change it!

HOME SWEET HOME?

'Those who don't believe in magic will never find it.'

Roald Dahl

Spending more time with the kids
had driven Valerie to drink and fags

Your life has constituent parts. In posh language, these are called 'domains' and to feel truly brilliant you need to be flourishing in all your domains. So, for example, you might be happy at work but not at home, in which case your overall life satisfaction will be hampered. Or vice versa.

> **Tip:** Men, when listening to your favourite CD, simply turn up the sound to the volume you desire – then turn it down three notches. This saves your wife having to do it.

And, without getting too technical, your domains can have domains! So, your 'happiness at work' can be subdivided into whether you're happy with your pay, job title, working hours, holidays, manager, etc. Once again, to feel at your best, the more domains that are sorted, the better! And it only takes one unsatisfactory 'domain' for your world to come crashing down.

This section of the book will take a cursory trawl through what we consider to be the two most important domains of your life, which are, in order of importance, 'home' and 'work'. There are tomes on 'parenting' and 'workplaces' that, quite frankly, we haven't got the expertise to compete with. But it's well worthwhile applying some of the themes we've already encountered and ramming the message home. Just like how the tea-pickers of Sri Lanka only pick the best leaves for your brew, we've chosen the snippets that are worth snipping.

First things first, your home domain.

'Happiness is having a large, loving, caring, close-knit family in another city.'

George Burns

I've already mentioned *Little House on the Prairie*, which is up there with *The Waltons* as the classic, clean-cut, wholesome family unit. I don't know about you, but our house doesn't resonate with a cheery '*Night Jim-Bob*' at lights out. And try as we might, we hardly ever manage to sit down around a huge table, slicing into and handing round generous helpings of hearty, home-made pumpkin pie. This isn't 1930s Walton Mountain. It's the next millennium along and it's Derby.

You can't avoid kids. Just to clarify, what I mean is you can take certain precautions to avoid *having* them, but you can't go through life without *encountering* them. Your own can be hard work. Other people's can be insufferable. We toyed with devoting a whole book to 'families' and that sits as a potential project for the future. For now, here's some headline news – stuff that will help you get on as a family unit.

'We got rid of the kids. The cat was allergic.'

Tee-shirt slogan

Recently, in my primary school workshops, I've started asking children this question: '*If you could take a pill that would make you happy forever, would you?*'

And I get a consistent answer. 'Don't be silly. Of course we wouldn't.'

Because, it seems, even among 9-year-olds, there's an appreciation that part of living a happy life is about acknowledging and experiencing sadness too. Yin and yang and all that. So, drop the banana of 'We must be happy at all times'. It's unrealistic.

But you can implement strategies that will enable your family to function brilliantly, *most* of the time. As Gretchen Rubin says, '*You're only as happy as your least happy child.*' So true!

While Carol Dweck's 'fixed' and 'growth' mind-set chapter is fresh in your minds, we may as well start there. I only scratched the surface of her research. She set the kids a really stern exam, after which one group was praised for intelligence ('*You are sooo clever!*') and the other for effort ('*You've worked reaaally hard!*').

Next, she set a test that was impossible for them to complete! For an 11-year-old, that's a real bummer. And here's the rub folks, the first group (praised for being clever) soon capitulated, figuring that they weren't clever enough. But the second group (praised for effort) stuck at it and outperformed the others by 30%.

So what?

Dweck's advice is that if your child accomplishes something, don't say, 'Well done, you are such a little genius!' But rather, 'Awesome, you put the effort in and got the reward.'

In a similar fashion, if your son scores a goal at football, don't high-five him and say, 'Holy cow, total genius dude. You were born to play football.'

You'd be better off saying, 'Amazing goal, son. That's what practice and hard work gets ya!' And ruffle his hair in a chummy fashion.

Or when your daughter wins an award for art, 'Crikey young lady, you are destined to be the next Picasso'? *Nope!* 'That's what you get for all those hours of hard work'? *Yep!*

The implications are profound at family level and even more staggering at school level. We tend to think that lowering standards will boost self-esteem and ultimately improve attainment. According to Dweck, '*lowering standards just leads to poorly educated students who feel entitled to easy work and lavish praise.*'

My wife slammed her fist on the table and said, 'Why must you question everything I say?

'*Everything?*' I replied.

And if you've got small children or grandchildren, here's another belter from Gretchen Rubin. You know how last thing at night can be a mad rush, dashing around getting school bags sorted, packed lunches packed and school uniforms ironed? Instead of rushing around, headless-chicken style, why not indulge in a spot of what she calls '*gazing lovingly*'. I think this is the most awesome thing I've shared with you in this book. Gretchen and her husband say, 'Come on, let's go and gaze lovingly at the kids as they sleep.'

That is such a fabulous idea.

Just a couple of riders though. Make sure they're your own kids. Breaking into next door's flat and gazing at *their* kids is never a great idea. Especially not lovingly!

And I think there's an age limit. It's perhaps best not to do this if you've got a 14-year-old son. If you enter his bedroom in the small hours, he will probably be gazing lovingly at something on the internet.

But, humour aside, it's a lovely concept. Simple, free and a perfect example of '*the beautiful ordinary*'.

And here's something else to consider – language. Geoff Miller tells us that adults have a vocabulary of approximately 60,000 words. Yet we use about 100 words for 60% of our conversations. And the most common words account for 98% of conversations!

So why do humans bother learning the extra 59,900 words? Geoff reckons it's to do with courtship! [32]

And if you visit proper academic papers and government reports, you'll find that far too many families are hindering their children's development. Language, as Alva Noë suggests, '. . . *is a shared cultural practice that can only be learned by a person who is one among many in a special kind of cultural eco-system.*' If you excuse the holier-than-thou terminology, Aloe Vera[33] argues that working-class homes tends to be quieter. There is much less spoken dialogue. The TV is on full time and not only are fewer words used, but the words have less variety.

A study by Hart and Risley (University of Kansas) suggested that by age 4, children raised in poor families will have heard 32

---

[32] *I've heard Andy W's chat-up lines and there are no words at all. Just a look and a grunt. That goes some of the way to explaining why he's single.*
[33] *Come on laugh. That's very funny.*

million *fewer* words than children raised in professional families. To add to the woe, it's not just quantity, it's also the emotional tone. Children can be bathed in approval and encouragement. Or the opposite!

I was in a school the other week and a 15-year-old boy confided that he'd never had a bedtime story read to him. I welled up. Nobody has ever thought it important enough to sit on the end of his bed and share *The Gruffalo*? (Or *Spy Dog*? I think that's what made me cry.)

When your children are small and they bring pictures home from nursery, you coo at their drawings and stick them proudly on the fridge door. You don't say, '*It's not your best work is it love? Get yourself up to your room and sharpen your pencils. You're not having any tea until you've coloured within the lines.*'

Although that scenario is faintly ridiculous, we do slip into the habit of telling children what they can't do. And if you're a new parent, I'd better warn you of what the established parents already know – your kids won't do what you say!

But they absolutely will do what you do!

So, when you're thinking of passing down your inheritance, be sure to remember that it's not just a lump of cash and a bit of jewellery. You are passing down habits, knowledge, explanatory styles and cognitive traits.

Carol Dweck (sorry to bang on about her, but she's done so much brilliant stuff!) speaks of 'dandelion' and 'orchid' children. If you're green fingered you'll appreciate that dandelion kids are even-tempered and hardy. They do pretty well wherever you put them. Whereas orchid kids are more variable. They can bloom spectacularly in the right setting or wither pitifully in the wrong one.

That's why parenting isn't an exact science!

Here's another pearler, this time from Dan Pink. I recommend his book, *Drive*, in which you'll find all sorts of thought-provoking ideas, but in terms of parenting, he says you shouldn't pay your kids to do chores and on no account should you bribe them with cash for exam results.

Whoops! I hear you say.

According to Dan, it's a slippery slope that kills their work ethic and love of learning. Let's examine the sub-text of your well-meaning exam 'payment by results' system, carefully devised in consultation with your teenager. What you are effectively saying is, '*I understand that studying is a horrible thing to do. And I appreciate that you will only do it for money.*'

Bang goes their love of learning. You are teaching them (albeit innocently and subconsciously) that learning is a chore.

Wowza! That's a gem folks. Instead you need to say, 'When you open that results envelope I want you to be proud of yourself. And we will be too!' Cheesy, but good.

> 'Those are my principles, and if you don't like them . . . well I have others.'
>
> Groucho Marx

Plus, one of the problems of bringing up teenagers is that hard work pays off in the future, whereas laziness pays off now. That's a really difficult one to get across to your kids without sounding like . . . *well* . . . their *dad!*

Think about what your kids see, hear and feel when you're around. What do you say at the end of the day?

'Everything that could go wrong did go wrong.'

Or, 'What a nightmare day.'

Or, 'Let me tell you how terrible my day's been.'

Or, 'Let me tell you about my amazing day.'

Or do you ask a really cool question like, 'What's the best thing that's happened to you at school today? Tell me about an amazing lesson or a funny incident'?

Don't fall into the trap of asking:

'How was school?'

'Boring!'

'What have you learned?'

'Can't remember!'

Let go of that particular communication banana. It's not working, so why continue to ask it?

Kim Cameron's superb book on *Positive Leadership* has so much cross-over with parenting.

He uses some big words, like 'affirmative bias' and 'heliotropic effect' but, at its heart, his principles are total genius. Put simply, an affirmative bias is an orientation towards your child's strengths rather than their weaknesses, optimism rather than pessimism and support rather than criticism.

And the heliotropic effect is 'the tendency of all living things to grow towards that which gives life and away from that which depletes life.'

In short, all living things have an inclination towards positivity. Plants lean towards the light. Kids lean towards encouragement. I'm struggling to find anything that I can say that is more enlightening than this.

Author in 'lost for words' conundrum!

Therefore, strategies that capitalise on the positive tend to produce life-giving, flourishing outcomes in individuals, families, schools and businesses. It's *THAT* simple.

Have we come full circle to Bob the effing Builder?

Please note, I'm not encouraging you to ignore negativity or weaknesses. It's also not about being Pollyannaish or nicey-nicey. Although, at its core, our approach is about being nice, it's about so much more than that. It's about supplementing your 'niceness' with strategies that promote strengths and energy.

Kim Cameron's work is about focusing on the kinds of things on the left of the list below:

What elevates you vs what challenges you.
What goes right vs what goes wrong.
What is life-giving vs what is life-depleting.
What is good vs what is objectionable.

What is extraordinary vs what is merely effective.
What is inspiring vs what is arduous.

In terms of 'orchids' and 'dandelions', the truth is that, as a parent, you are having an *extraordinary* effect on the climate at home. I can't think of anything more important you'll ever do than re-create the heliotropic effect. That's what Ma and Pa Walton did. And it's most definitely what Charles Ingells from *The Little House on the Prairie* did.

And just to square this bumper section off, I have to tell you about 'The Matthew Effect', another little-known but hugely profound line of academia.

The Matthew Effect is when an initial success in something leads to even greater success. And, conversely, if we are unsuccessful, we're likely to become even more unsuccessful. In short, it seems that success and failure will grow like Topsy, whichever gets the upper hand. The effect derives its name from a passage in the Gospel of St Matthew, 25:29. '*To everyone who has, will more be given, and he will have abundance. But from him who has not, even what he has will be taken away.*'

Heavy stuff, but most probably true. Let me give you just one example – children who start off reading well will get better and better compared to their peers, because they will read even more broadly and quickly. The more words they learn, the easier and more enjoyable it becomes. On the other hand, it's very hard for poor readers to catch up, because, for them, the spiral goes downwards.

Due to The Matthew Effect, the gap between those who read well and those who read poorly grows even bigger rather than smaller.

That's The Matthew Effect: success snowballs, but so does failure. It's why the rich get richer and the poor poorer. This means it's vital to get our upward spiral going in the right direction at an early age.

Recently I had the privilege of working with a fantastic group of people. They were all troubled, some by alcohol, some by drugs, some by domestic or child abuse. Most had, at some point, slept on the streets. Their CVs weren't overburdened with qualifications, there were a few mental health issues thrown in and their track records were, at best, grim. On a confidence scale of 1–10, most were a zero. In terms of The Matthew Effect, I think it's fair to say their lives had the trajectory of a bullet-ridden Spitfire.

So we set about delivering 'The Art of Being Brilliant', tailored to fit their circumstances and with fingers and toes tightly crossed. This was a huge test for them and us. Three days later, we had some big results. I will spare you the specifics, but suffice to say that with a little encouragement, a modicum of common sense, a few tears (mine and theirs!), some hard work and a few laughs, these wonderful people started to realise just how wonderful they really are.

They left, their lights burning brighter. And I left, thinking of The Matthew Effect. I'll remember them all forever. But Becky stands out. She has two young boys. And when I asked her what she would do differently as a result of coming on the course, she said she'd make sure that her sons would grow up positive and confident, improving their life chances. And she meant it.

Matthew Effect, are you listening? You owe Becky an upward spiral.

A BRIEF INTERLUDE FOR SOME 'MARS AND VENUS' STUFF

Gladys reminded Harold, "Before we make love could you put out the bins?"

Families aren't just about kids. There are grown-ups involved too. Here's a soupcon of gender generalisation that might just save your relationship.

If women are asked to describe their ideal man, they'll usually end up describing another woman. They'll go all misty-eyed and describe their perfect man as '*Caring and thoughtful. Someone who knows how I feel.*' And, above all, '*Someone who listens.*'

Pardon?

Now, I'm not a male apologist, but the truth is that men and women are wired differently. And when I say 'differently' I mean men are wired 'more simply'.

Female brains are like spaghetti junction with criss-crossing highways and by-ways of fast-moving emotional traffic. Blokes are more like the A458 heading out of Shrewsbury on a Sunday morning. Quiet and uncluttered.

Men are able to compartmentalise. They have little boxes in their brains. A work box. A shed box. A partner box. A watching-the-football box, and such like. One of the boxes contains nothing. And I mean absolutely diddly-squat, bugger-all emptiness. So, if you ask a man what he's thinking and he says, 'nothing', he's absolutely correct. And the absurd thing is that women can't think of 'nothing' in the same manner. They can think about things that aren't worth thinking about, but they can't think of 'nothing'.

It must be awful, what with all that noise?

Men and women are men and women for a reason. Stop pretending we're the same. Here's a top tip for each gender.

Fact (this information is for males only)
At least 15% of human *females* possess a genetic mutation that gives them an extra (fourth) photoreceptor. This allows them to discriminate between colours that look identical to the average male. So, when you have a fashion dilemma and you seek a second opinion, do what all males do – hold up the clothes and let her choose.

'The shirt in your left hand, cos it's got a fleck of blue so will match your trousers.'

You look at the shirt that you'd previously thought to be green. *Blue? Is it? Really?*

Yes it is. Wear it.

Fact (this information is for females only)
Women have superior brains and something called 'retrachromic vision'. It enables you to distinguish between colours that men just don't see. All men see in only 16 colours. 'Peach', for example, is a fruit, not a colour. So is 'pumpkin'.

And we have no idea what 'mauve' is.

Thank you.

I'M HERE, ALL WEAK

'It's nigh on impossible to be half a person at work and a full person outside.'

Nigel Marsh

Little did they know it, but if they all worked together they could totally f**k the system

This isn't a business book. But 'work' is likely to be one of your main 'domains'. In fact, the chances are you spend more time with your work colleagues than your family, so it's worth unearthing a few nuggets and exploring a few ideas that will help you to flourish at work.

The first thing to realise is that you can change your job while you're still in it. By applying some of the thinking outlined in the earlier chapters, you can flick a switch in your head and decide to be the best employee they've ever had. You really can.

Harry Emerson Fosdick famously wrote about a summer's day during his childhood when his mother sent him out to pick a quart of raspberries. 'I dragged my feet in rebellion,' he said, 'and the bucket was filling very slowly. Then a new idea came to me. Wouldn't it be fun to pick two quarts of raspberries and surprise her?'

So the young lad set about his new task. 'I had such an interesting time picking those two quarts, to the utter amazement of the household, and they never forgot it. But I have never forgotten the philosophy of it. We can change any situation by changing our attitude toward it. Nobody ever finds life worth living. One always has to make it worth living.'

From an early age we absorb the fact that 'work' is a necessary evil. Horrid Henry hints at it. Bart and Homer reinforce it. *Doh!*

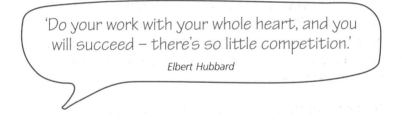

'Do your work with your whole heart, and you will succeed – there's so little competition.'

Elbert Hubbard

But you might not need to flick that switch in your head. It depends on whether you're employed in a job, career or a calling.

If you're doing a 'job', you'll feel it in the pit of your stomach. Going to work will be a chore. You're doing it because it pays the bills and you get that feeling of angst when the alarm goes off at stupid o'clock.

'I hate my supervisor. Behind her desk it says, "You don't have to be mad to work here, but it helps." Mind you, she's written it in her own shit.'

Alan Carr

A 'career' is a necessity, but you see opportunities for success and advancement. It's up the evolutionary scale from a 'job' and you're likely to feel you're moving in the right direction. You're invested in your work and want to do well.

A 'calling' is where the work is the end in itself. You feel fulfilled and have a sense of contribution to the greater good. Work is likely to draw on your personal strengths and gives your life meaning and purpose. And, whisper it quietly, *you'd probably do it for free.*

Whether you're engaged in a job, a career or a calling has less to do with your work than you might imagine. A calling orientation can have just as much to do with your mind-set as it does with the actual work being done. Harry's 'quart of raspberries' story is an example of how deciding to do something with gusto can change the nature of the task from a 'job' to a 'calling'.

This links with Simon Sinek's amazingly simple concept of the 'Golden Circle'. His model is represented below.

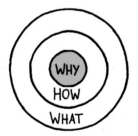

Most organisations start at the outside of the circle and work inwards. So, for example, I'd expect every member of your organisation to know *what* their job is. Most large organisations lay this down in a job description, giving you reams of detail that explain exactly what is expected of you. *Yawn!*

Check this out by David 'Naked Leader' Taylor. It's about Service Level Agreements and, I ask you, has there ever been a better piece of business writing?

See how effective 'Service Level Agreements' are for yourself.

Tonight, persuade your partner to cook you a meal – eat it, while saying nothing – show no expression whatsoever.

When you have finished and your chef asks – 'Did you enjoy it?'

Reply – 'It was satisfactory.'

And later – if you still have a relationship, and after enjoying some romantic, intimate moments together – your partner whispers in your ear: 'How was it for you?'

Pause for a few moments, look them right in the eyes, and say: 'you met my expectations.'

Protocols, job descriptions, Service Level Agreements, personal specifications . . . the whole shebang is ludicrous!

Back to Sinek's Golden Circle, you know *what* you're supposed to be doing and, if you're lucky, your employer will furnish you with the tools to get on with the 'how' bit. That might be a desk and a laptop and a kitchen to brew your tea. Or a van and some tools and a mobile phone.

The more switched-on businesses will get to grips with the 'why' bit. In fact, the *really* switched-on businesses will start with the 'why' because if employees have a clear and compelling 'why', the 'how' and 'what' will look after themselves. Indeed, for those employees who have no fire in their belly, the chances are they have either forgotten or never had their 'why'.

201

Why do you get out of bed in the morning? *Why* do you go to work? If you're struggling with valid reasons, you're guaranteed to be struggling to get out of bed on a dark winter's morning.

Here are some interesting questions that will guide you towards your 'why?'

- What is your purpose?
- What are you aiming for?
- What holds most meaning for you?

This is a crucial golden thread that links me back to my earlier suggestion that maybe we are disguising 'busy' as 'purpose'. Or *substituting* 'busy' for 'purpose' when, deep down, we know we are missing a clear and compelling 'why?'

This takes me into a whole depth of territory that I'm not qualified for. I'd need a rope and hard hat to be lowered that deep and, quite frankly, I don't know what's down there. I asked Andy W for an opinion at this point and he just scratched his head, not even understanding the question. But it might well be one of the reasons that research consistently correlates religion and happiness. If religion gives a higher meaning, then it stands to reason that there will be links to happiness. However, your 'meaning' or your 'why' or your 'purpose' doesn't have to come from God.

Andy W's came from Mr Warren. Most people at some point in their life have worked for a boss or had a teacher who brought out the best in them. They managed to stretch you outside of your comfort zone and produce better results than you ever thought you were capable of. Quite often, this person will have had more faith in you than you had in yourself.

Andy W's maths teacher, Mr Warren, was one of those people. As far as we know, he wasn't God. Andy describes him as old-school, ex RAF with the stereotypical big moustache and a deep, scary voice. He was the kind of teacher that most students listened to out of fear. Andy's maths hadn't been going well due to the fact that he didn't really give a shit. He tells me, and I don't quite know why it's so funny, *'Why should I care about how many oranges Bhupindra's supposed to have?'*

All the other teachers had failed to engage my esteemed co-author, so he ended up in the last-chance saloon, Mr Warren's class. And, you've guessed it, Andy was asked to stay behind after the very first lesson.

Mr Warren sat Andy down and said, 'Whittaker, I don't care what the other teachers say about you. You remind me of me when I was your age. I was a dickhead back then as well.' (He had a way with words did Mr Warren.) 'I messed up my schooling and had to go back to college to get my exams, which was a pain in the arse. I held myself back in my career at least five years. I don't want that for you. I see something special in you and I don't want you to waste a single drop of your talent. If you want, we will get you through maths together.'

He held his hand out for Andy to shake, which he duly did. Maths was one of the few exams Andy passed and he will remember Mr Warren for the rest of his days.

Why?

Andy didn't want to let him down. He had a reason to come to maths. His 'why' was sorted.

Tip: Follow the 45/5 rule. Only work 45 hours. And 5 of those are for self-development (curled up in bed reading this book, and being paid for it!)

Simon Sinek weaves a compelling argument that the majority of great leaders, the people who have made a real difference in the world such as the Wright brothers, Dr Martin Luther King, John F. Kennedy and, more recently, Steve Jobs, Bill Gates and Richard Branson, all started with a compelling 'why'.

But you don't have to be Gandhi to have a brilliant 'why'. Your 'why' can be 'to make a difference' or 'to go the extra mile for my colleagues' or 'to provide some positivity at work.'

Rodney had decided to give 100% at work.

12% on Monday
23% on Tuesday
40% on Wednesday
20% on Thursday
5% on Friday

Let me give you a chilling example of someone who has lost their way.

This is painfully true, to the point of being disturbing. I once sat through a meeting with a child protection team where there had been some serious failings. The old boss had been 'let go' and the new chief was attempting to draw a line in the sand. The team's failings had resulted in the death of a child and the inquest was about to be splashed all over the news. This, folks, was not some minor misdemeanour, it was serious, grade-A shit.

I listened as the new leader did an impassioned speech. I was choked up. The mitigating circumstances were that the team was overwhelmed with pressure, stretched to the point that they had broken. I could see both sides. But, however you looked at it, there was no escaping the fact that a series of oversights had resulted in a terrible tragedy. The new leader finished her speech. That particular department was about to be harangued in the national press the very next day. Let me reiterate, their errors had resulted in the death of a child.

The new boss finished her speech and looked across at the stony silence of 60 people. 'Any questions?'

'Yes,' said a poker-faced lady. 'You've cut our mileage rate to 35p. I, for one, will not be visiting any more homes, unless by bus.'

And I sat there, slack-jawed. A job that I had assumed was a calling, was, to her, a job. She'd lost her 'why'. Or maybe she'd never had it in the first place.

To this day, I feel crushed by her comment.

I doubt she started out like that. She'd allowed herself to *become* like that. It makes me (and I'm hoping you too) determined to avoid becoming that salary-chasing, passionless, hardened, finger-pointing, unmanageable cynic.

'EXTRAORDINARY' AS STANDARD

'I know I used to be somebody, but I can't remember who.'

Mr Nobody

Stella had decided she wasn't weird.
She was 'limited edition'.

In a previous chapter, we spoke about values. But business values don't work in the same way as personal values. Let me give you an example; here are some awesome business values:

* integrity
* communication
* respect
* excellence.

And they belong to . . . *Enron!* An organisation, in case you've forgotten, that was corrupt to its core.

'Bad companies are the abattoirs of the human soul.'
Nigel Marsh

My point being that you can talk about 'values' until the cows come home. And the pigs and sheep too if you like. But values aren't to be talked about. They're to be lived. In fact, I think if you're having to have a meeting about 'values', you've probably missed the point. People don't live business values, they live their own.

Here's my nagging feeling – positive psychology is the right philosophy but for the wrong reasons. We're using the science of happiness and wellbeing to create workplaces that are engaging and fun, where people can feel great. *Yippee!*

With the underlying business mantra that they will therefore work harder and make more profit for you. And while this makes perfect sense at one level, treating people well because it's good for your profits is the wrong reason for treating them well.

Treating your people well because that's absolutely the right thing to do. That's where enlightened workplaces position themselves.

I am certain that the vast majority of employees come to work wanting to do a great job. I promise you, they're gagging to do their best. They are desperate to feel valued and respected.

As a parent, you rectify your child's mistakes with love and care. You show your child a better way. In organisations, when someone makes a mistake, a policy is put in place to ensure it never happens again.

Every time you put a policy, protocol or procedure into your organisation, you take away some passion and trust from the people who are already doing the job.

Why do organisations punish their brilliant staff members for the mistakes of their rubbish ones? Invariably, rules, procedures and standards are there to stop people being rubbish. The problem is they also clip the wings of those who are brilliant!

Keep putting new policies and standards in place, keep looking at the figures and one day you will find all the passion and trust has gone. And isn't *passion* the reason why the organisation started in the first place?

Let me give you a couple of real-world examples. I recently ran a session for some graduate nurses. The whole thing was set against the backdrop of a government report insinuating that *'nurses don't care'*. In itself, that seems a ridiculous sentence.

So, without it being overtly said to me, the brief was, 'Andy, you've got a day. Can you get them to care?'

I can't ever remember working with a group of people who cared *soooo* much. They were inspired and inspiring and their caring cups were spilling over. They didn't need training up. They needed the NHS to stop putting up ridiculous barriers that were blocking their awesomeness!

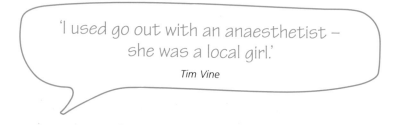

'I used go out with an anaesthetist – she was a local girl.'

Tim Vine

Plus, from another business sector comes this all-too-common example of misguided customer service. My car was in for a service and the garage phoned me to inform me I'd be needing an oil change (my car needed it actually, not me, but you know what I mean). 'Fair enough,' I said, 'but why are you asking me?'

'Well sir, do you want a *normal* oil change or do you want to pay extra and have a *proper* oil change? With *special* oil!'

I beg your pardon? My answer is probably the same as everyone else's answer. I want a *proper* effing oil change and I don't want to pay extra. I want it done brilliantly. I don't want a second-class service.

Imagine, on being wheeled into the operating theatre, a nurse asking you, 'Do you want a *proper* appendectomy? Or do you want a half-hearted approach where we leave the forceps in?'

I want *extraordinary*, first time, every time. And, frustratingly, this seems beyond most organisations. All too often, the organisation is getting in the way of its people.

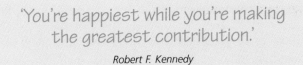

'You're happiest while you're making the greatest contribution.'

Robert F. Kennedy

But a handful really do get it. One of our happiness legends is Tony Hsieh (pronounced 'Shay'), chief executive at an American company, Zappos. If you follow Tony's story, he elevated his company into the billion-dollar-turnover category by making it a great place to work. He puts 'happiness' as the central tenet. His view is that you can't browbeat, bully or bribe people to be happy. They have to feel it for themselves. Crucially, we believe Tony is doing it for the *right* reasons.

Of course, Zappos has its sceptics. Maybe Tony is just plain lucky. Maybe his idea of selling shoes via the web was just the right idea at the right time and therefore destined for greatness even if he had treated his staff like mushrooms.[34]

---

[34] *i.e. kept them in the dark and fed them shit.*

Instead of measuring the call centre on 'calls answered per minute', he insists that the operators be trained and rewarded to take their time and actually be human, to connect and make a difference instead of merely reading from a script and processing the call.

And here's the best bit about Zappos. After your two-week induction, Tony offers new staff $2000 to *leave*. Take it or leave it, no catch, no hard feelings, you can have the money and run. Or, alternatively, if you *really* want to work for us, stay and join a rocking team that achieves results through being happy first.

We reckon Tony's got a clear and compelling 'why'. And we're fairly sure that Tony's employees know what their 'why' is too.

Tony understands that his employees are already motivated when they join his business. Whereas most managers think their role is to 'motivate' their employees, Tony has cottoned on to the fact that he has to stop doing the things that strip away motivation. Humans have an inherent drive to do well. *Get out of their bloody way!*

Happiness, positivity and 'buzz' are viral things. As a researcher, I'm interested in tipping points. How many positive people do you need before it becomes socially contagious?

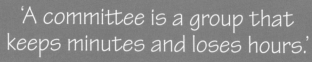

'A committee is a group that keeps minutes and loses hours.'
Milton Berle

Traditional organisational change programmes (*yawn, again!*) are about strategy, planning, distributing tasks, communication, training . . . and, if you're lucky, change is squeezed out at the end. But invariably it's a long, hard process.

Viral change is pretty cool because it's about sustaining new *thinking* and *behaviours* rather than processes. It has more in common with fashion or a YouTube video that gets a billion hits. You don't shoot a video and stick it on YouTube *expecting* it to go viral. The word gets around and it just takes off.

Rather than command and control, this is more about influencing people to *want* to change. It feels more natural. 'Why?' is firmly at the core. The focus is on changing the meaning. If people have meaning, their behaviours will change. People will simply 'catch' the new behaviours. Doesn't that sound a lot easier than forcing change through?

> 'People want to be a part of an organization that lets them be fully alive and bring their gifts to work.'
>
> *Robin Sharma*

With your good grace, I'd like to remind you of the *4-minute rule*, a concept put forward by Steve McDermott, and something that we featured in our previous book. Some things are so brilliant that they bear repeating. In essence, the 4-minute rule suggests that it takes four minutes for other people to 'catch' your feelings. So, if you're upbeat, passionate and positive for four minutes, the people around you will have almost no choice but to feel good too.

I have to say, it's the most remarkable, simple and do-able concept I've ever encountered. I practise it at home and at work. It's sublime because what it's really suggesting is that you don't have to be brilliant forever – just for four minutes! And anyone can do that . . . *can't they?*

Back to the theme of viral change, which involves the spreading of attitudes and behaviours. Obviously, if positivity is to spread, it needs to be visible. So here's an interesting thought, what if you're happy on the inside but it doesn't show on the outside?

Here's an example of the 4-minute rule. I won't name the company; suffice to say that I worked with the senior management team and a couple of days after I'd delivered 'The Art of Being Brilliant', the top bloke rang me up and said, 'Andy, it's not working.'

'Waddayamean?'

'I mean, I'm happy on the inside but it doesn't show on the outside. People aren't noticing. It's not going viral.'

This was going to be a long conversation, so I took the phone from my hot ear and stuck it on speakerphone. 'Have you tried smiling?' I suggested, without wanting to sound overly patronising.

'Smiling?' he repeated. I could picture him scratching his head. 'It's not really, you know, what I do. I feel great but other people aren't catching it. So can you come and follow me around for a day and give me some advice?'

So I did. I turned up on Monday morning, clipboard in hand, a man on a mission. I've got one day to turn him into an inspirational leader. Except, I didn't need a day. *I needed four minutes*. Let me explain. Our hero was a big cheese. A big enough cheese to warrant a Monday morning meeting of all department heads, which he chaired. I settled in at the back, pencil licked, ready to scribble.

I observed my protagonist. If owners look like their dogs, I'll wager he's got a bloodhound.

Our hero sat there, slumped and lifeless with a hang-dog expression. *He's not just a bloodhound, he's a depressed bloodhound.* He kept looking down at the agenda (*his* agenda!) and sighing. There were several audible tutts, some pursing of lips and a couple of minor headshakes as the members of the senior team took their seats. It was boardroom style, and our man was at the head of the table. So, as everyone entered, their attention naturally gravitated to the leader.

'Are we all here?' he said, glancing up and puffing out his cheeks. 'I hope your weekend's been better than mine. It was shit. Anyway, here we go again,' he sighed. 'Another Monday meeting. The agenda looks a bit heavy,' he complained, 'but if there are no questions, we could be out in an hour. So let's kick off. Agenda item number 1 . . . reported accidents and near misses since the last meeting . . .'

And, to his credit, exactly an hour later the meeting finished. There was some grinding of chairs as his managers stood and silently left the room, every ounce of energy extracted from them. If you've ever seen a zombie movie you'll know what I mean. They staggered, heavy limbed, back to their offices to spread the Monday morning woe.

And our hero looked up at me, quivering in my seat, and asked, 'Any tips? Is there anything I could have done differently?'

'What? Apart from *everything!*' I said, unable to mask my incredulity. I was aware that he was happy on the inside and I didn't want to piss on that particular fire. 'You're the leader. You have to lead by example. If you want your team to be inspired, you have to be inspired. And I mean *visibly* inspired.'

I went to the door. 'What if you, *the leader*, had been waiting at the door, grinning and shaking their hands as they entered. "I hope you've had a brill weekend. Sit yourself down. We've got so much good stuff to get through this morning. I can't wait to get started." '

He was looking a little bemused.

'And, once they're all in, sit in your seat.' I plonked myself at the head of the table. 'But sit down like an 8-year-old on Christmas Eve. Don't settle. Be excited. Edge of your seat. Don't start straight away. Let them natter with their fellow managers for a minute or two. All you have to do is sit there, occasionally glancing down at the agenda, mouthing "*wow*" and scribbling a few last-minute notes.'

He was nodding. 'And then, eventually, you begin, enthusiastically, with something like, "Great to see you all again. I hope you've had a terrific weekend? I can't believe we're here again! The start of another *awesome* week. Another opportunity to wow our customers . . ." '

He was grimacing as if that might be a step too far, so I turned it down a notch. 'I've worked here 10 years and have never seen an agenda this exciting,' I beamed. 'But before we start, I want to spend a couple of minutes with you sharing the best example of customer service you've seen in your team since the last meeting.'

Our hero was back on board with me. He was nodding and, dare I say it, showing some outward sign of happiness, an enthusiastic grin lighting up his face. Bloodhound had been replaced by Labrador. 'And once they've shared best practice, the room will be buzzing and you hit them with "agenda item number 1: health and safety good news . . ." '

The Labrador looked like he was on the promise of walkies. His tongue wasn't quite lolloping out, but it wasn't far off. 'And an hour later, they're skipping back to their teams. Invigorated and inspired.'

Our senior management Labrador was now so excited I thought he might start humping my leg in appreciation. *Down boy!* 'Same meeting, same people, same agenda,' I reminded. 'But a different first four minutes.'

You can't get simpler than that. He'd learned to go viral, four minutes at a time.

'One person with passion is better than forty people merely interested.'

E. M. Forster

Marty figured his past was fully booked so he'd gamble on there being a vacancy in his future

I read the following paragraph, written by an esteemed author:

> Each and every one of us harbours the illusion that the whole enterprise would go straight to hell without our individual daily contributions. In fact no one is indispensable. Every worker is replaced and forgotten as swiftly as the anonymous slaves who hauled blocks for the pyramids.

And I thought, how far off the mark can you be? Sure, there are some colleagues who, if they found jobs elsewhere, you could replace easily. But, there are others who you could never replace. Look around your workplace. There are people who are worth their weight in gold. They don't necessarily have the sharpest intellect nor are they necessarily the most talented, but they are adding a certain something, that something being enthusiasm, energy, buzz, positivity and a 'can do' mentality. They are great to have around because they give everyone else a lift. These people are what I call 2%ers – the small elite of genuinely positive people who make the world go round. They create upward spirals of enthusiasm and energy in the people around them. Spookily, they do this at home too.

This entire book has been about 2%ers. I just haven't mentioned the phrase![35]

Eventually, you will move on from your current job. And I want your colleagues to mourn. I really do! I want them to miss your energy and cheeriness. Ask yourself, '*What have I got to do to have them talking glowingly about me five years after I've left?*'

And do it!

---

[35] *Yes, this is a blatant plug for our first book,* The Art of Being Brilliant, *which explains the six principles that will transform you into a 2%er.*

BONUS STORY

Monsters Inc.

If you've seen *Monsters Inc.* you'll know it's a cool movie. If you haven't seen it . . . what are you waiting for?

Sully is a blue, hairy hulk of a monster. His buddy, Mike, is well . . . an eye. On legs. And they are a team. They work for 'Monsters Incorporated', a huge organisation that employs monsters to scare children into screaming. They then bottle the screams to create electricity that powers their city (Monstropolis . . . where else?).

The children are scared of the monsters and, interestingly, the monsters have been taught to be scared of the children. Cue a superb link to 'beliefs' and 'fixed mind-sets'. With me so far?

Except Sully messes up big time. The big blue buffoon accidentally brings a child back to Monstropolis. And he finds that the child (Boo) is a sweet, innocent thing. And Boo has no fear of Sully. I guess she's not *learned* to be scared. The breakthrough comes when Mike and Sully discover that Boo's laughter also creates energy. And then it's a good, old-fashioned battle between the old way (creating fear) versus the new way (creating happiness).

It's such a great idea for a movie. And the clincher is when they discover that laughter has 10 times more power than fear. *Imagine!* So the monsters have to change their approach, adopting silly hats and churning out smiles instead of roars. It seems the new way is more powerful than the old.

And I can't help thinking it's the best *business documentary* ever made!

4000 WEEKS . . .

'There is no such thing as a happy ending. Every culture has a maxim that makes this point, while nowhere in the universe is there a single gravestone that reads, "He Loved Everything About His Life, Especially the Dying Bit at the End".'

Douglas Adams

There's a small settlement in the north of New Zealand called Whitianga and, apparently, as you drive into town there's a sign that says '*Slow Down, You're Here*'.

I reckon that's a perfect way to start this final chapter. In fact, I'm tempted to stop writing, right now. I doubt I can find a better conclusion than that.

But I can't leave without sharing this story . . .

Argentinian golfer, Roberto de Vincenzo, won a tournament and the big cheque that goes with it. After the celebrations, he was strolling back to his car when he was approached by a young woman who congratulated him on his victory. She told him her daughter was seriously ill and close to death. She needed an expensive heart operation.

Roberto didn't think twice. He took out his pen and signed the cheque over to the woman.

At next week's tournament, a golfing official approached Roberto and said he'd heard the winner's cheque had been given away. 'I have bad news,' he said. 'It was a con. You've been duped. There is no sick child. She's fleeced you.'

'You mean there is no baby who is dying?' said Roberto.

'That's right,' said the golf official, shaking his head.

'That's the best news I've heard all week!'

A silly story? Or a profoundly moving example of how to change your thinking to get yourself a much better result? Your call.

I have an admission – this book was the publisher's idea. Andy and I wrestled with the notion for a while before we said 'yes'. And, here's another admission that might sound a little trite, but we started with the 'why?'

And we came to the conclusion that our 'why?' was to share some information that we genuinely think will make a difference to the people who can be bothered to read it. Our 'why' was to *remind* you of how awesome you already are, when you're functioning at your best. If we could made you chuckle too, that'd be a bonus.

'I want to die peacefully in my sleep, like my granddad. Not screaming and yelling like his passengers.'

Bob Monkhouse

Our second big question was where to pitch it? I'm proud to say that our previous book was almost universally well received and, like most ego-driven authors, we trawl through the Amazon reviews. Positive reviews make us glow. Negative reviews make us question why we bother!

So we then do what all other authors do, we compare our reviews with the reviews of our heroes' books. And, get this, even our heroes get negative reviews! That's astonishing. Even the best self-help books in the universe get panned. There are a lot of miserable people out there who read the personal development genre and then take to Amazon to say the books are too simple or that they didn't work. So I thought I'd nail those two points up front in an attempt to head criticism off at the pass.

Firstly, for those who think this book is too simple. *Excellent*. That's exactly what we set out to do. Unravelling the already simple science of feeling good to the level of the bleeding obvious – that was our mission.

And don't go moaning that this book is the same as all the other self-help books, because it isn't. You'd never heard of '*Vipassana Vendetta*' until you read this book and you'd not used the word '*heliotrope*' ever. '*Umwelt*' and '*umgebung*' have never been part of your vocabulary either, OK? We've also explained why you feel great when you're standing atop a hill. Plus there is no other book on the planet in which someone from Mansfield has grappled with quantum physics. For that chapter alone, it deserves a 5-star review!

Secondly, for those who read our book and dismiss it because it doesn't work, we haven't really offered reams of 'advice', as such. It's more of a 'mind manual', a bit like the old-fashioned Haynes car repair manuals. Dead simple.

This book will not make you happier or more positive. This book will not change your life. Unless, of course, you put some effort into implementing some (or all) or the concepts we talk about. Taking no action is easy. We are calling for sustained effort and practice folks. Your Haynes manual didn't work while it was sat on your bookshelf, but it was invaluable when you were tinkering under the bonnet.

Tinkering? 'The Tinker Man?' Isn't that where we came in?

Remember the TV programme, *Bullseye*? It was a darts game-show, circa 1980s, hosted by the indomitable Jim Bowen. Jim was unquestionably the best game-show host in the history of TV land. He had umpteen catchphrases but he always saved the best till last. When you lost (which contestants invariably did), Jim would shuffle centre stage and announce, 'Never mind lads, let's see what you *could* have won.'

And the stage would rotate to reveal a tantalising Ford Fiesta, caravan or speed boat. It was pure genius as the camera cut away, with Jim beaming and his contestants ashen faced.

And exactly 10 years from today, I'm going to track you down. Mark it on your calendar right now. I'm going to ask WHSmith for the name and address of everyone who's ever bought this book. I know where you live! And I'll come knocking at your door. You'll answer and there I'll be, clipboard in hand and Jim Bowen grin on my face. 'Hi there, it's me, one of the authors of the "brilliant" book. May I ask you, how have your 10 years been?'

And if you look down at your furry slippers and sigh, 'Nightmare!' I will become Jim bloody Bowen.

'Well isn't that sad,' I'll say. 'Let's look at the life you could have won.'

> 'If you met yourself at a party would you want to strike up a conversation?'
>
> *Unknown*

So here's my final thought. Everyone needs heroes. But for society to flourish we need the right kind of heroes. I feel the pendulum might have swung towards celebrity for the sake of itself. For 'hero' read 'celebrity'. And for 'celebrity' read *vacuous orange person with boob job and collagen lips, from a reality show, probably in Essex*.

This book isn't about *what* you want to be. The subliminal question throughout has been, '*what kind of person do you want to be?*'

Let me remind you that the average lifespan in the UK is about 4000 weeks. I want you to be a superhero for however many of those weeks you've got left. Not the vacuous reality-TV kind of hero, more the jaw-dropping 'made of positive stuff' kind.

'Heliotrope Woman', a hero to her children and grandchildren. A shining light to her work colleagues and a beacon of positivity to whomever she meets. You need to say that in a deep, movie-trailer voice. It has a nice ring to it.

But, of course, being a superhero takes a bit of effort. It's a lot easier to be . . .

'Bog-Standard Man', striving for mediocrity and the weekends, living a luke-warm life and spreading averageness wherever he goes. Even with the voice that doesn't sound nearly as good.

And the truth is that we can't do it for you. The most important point is that *you* need to *want* to be a superhero too!

'*How we spend our days,*' Annie Dillard once wrote, '*is, of course, how we spend our lives.*' Our lives are a chain of these days. We grow, or we stagnate. We can form good habits or destructive ones. Or, more often than not, *both*. We learn from our mistakes, or we keep repeating them until we're in enough pain to make changes.

'He stared at the gorgeous countryside whilst leaning against the door of his car. He had some important decisions to make. His smart-phone was making him stupid; that was for sure. His satnav was causing him to lose his sense of direction. His microwave was removing his love of food. E-mail was damaging good relationships. Box-sets were wrecking his love-life. And the heated driver's seat was making him soft.'

Nicholas Bate

I can think back through my years and trace a path to where I am now. But there is no straight arrow pointing from '*teenager with greasy hair and denim jacket*' to '*middle-aged man tapping away at laptop*'.

Life isn't a simple game of dot-to-dot. I doubt you have a plan. I'm not absolutely sure that I have. Life isn't as smooth as '*A leads to B and then to C . . . and you die at Z.*'

Life is a scribbly scrawl of a line. It can look a right bloody mess!

But if I could reach back through time and whisper something to that denim-clad youth with the poster of the bare-bottomed tennis lady on his bedroom wall, it would simply be this:

'*Be patient. Be kind to yourself. And wake up.*'

ABOUT ANDY AND ANDY

Andy Whittaker is a trainer, author and joker. He loves people. Posh ones, rough ones, male, female, fat, slim, all colours, ages and sexual preferences. He used to be irritated by negative people, but recently decided that life's too short. He's not very good at writing, so is thankful to the other Andy for helping out.

Andy Cope is an author, trainer and learning junkie. His love of learning didn't kick in until his mid-30s, so he's making up for lost time. As well as studying for a PhD, Andy is also a children's author and that, dear reader, is a very jarring juxtaposition. Andy isn't very funny, so he's thankful to the other Andy for helping out.

Andy and Andy have teamed up with a few like-minded trainers to run 'Brilliant' workshops for businesses and schools across the world. The messages are gleaned from Andy C's PhD, but great care is taken to extract the big words and deliver the messages in a simple and engaging way. The workshops also happen to be fab fun.

Feel free to check us out at www.artofbrilliance.co.uk

Thank you.

Acknowledgements

We have been influenced and inspired by so many wonderful people. Some are obvious; some less so. Many won't even be aware of the impact they've had.

If your name appears on this list, you've played a part in helping us write this book. We are truly grateful . . .

Andy Cope would like to thank Darrell Woodman, Simon Sinek, Shawn Achor, David Hyner, Richard Gerver, the Capstone team, David 'Naked Leader' Taylor, Paul 'SUMO' McGee, Sir John Jones, Nigel Marsh, Bob the Builder, Kav Vaseer, Kev House, Seth Godin, Jack Pransky, Dr Robert Holden, Philip Ardagh, Dan Rockwell, Jonathan Haidt, the lads from 1976 (Pat, Ju, Mick, Woody, Bell, Bail), Nigel Percy, David Wilkin, Carol Dweck, Richard Wilkins, Kim Cameron, Robin Sharma, Barbara Fredrickson, Paul McKenna, Winn Claybaugh, Stuart Spendlow, Nicholas Bate, Lou and Laura Maddox.

Andy Whittaker would like to thank Craig, Wendy, Harvey, Ollie McNab, Benjamin, Samuel and Millie Ford, The Hallams, Rigbys, Crawleys, Fosters, Roses, Cheesmonds, Popes, Cundalls, Mystic Tina, Mystic Meryl, Jonsey, Bayliss, Nudge, Mickey, Flacky, Festival Mark, Tilly, Barry at the Fountain, the lads at the Meat Larder, everyone who worked at the Halifax Building Society in Lancaster when my Dad worked there, Dummy and The Powell, Bobby and Byro, Sammy and Ben. And to all the girls I've loved before.

Also available from
ANDY COPE & ANDY WHITTAKER
A title to help people live brilliant lives,
be successful and be happy

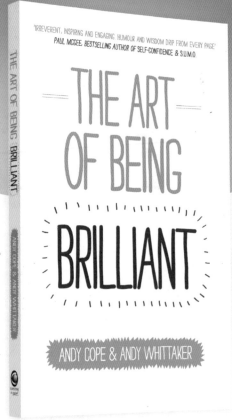

'IRREVERENT, INSPIRING AND ENGAGING. HUMOUR AND WISDOM DRIP FROM EVERY PAGE'
PAUL MCGEE, BESTSELLING AUTHOR OF SELF-CONFIDENCE & S.U.M.O.

THE ART
OF BEING

BRILLIANT

ANDY COPE & ANDY WHITTAKER